For Valorie —
with special
blessings,
Marcus Bach
4/16/67

The
Unity
Way of Life

BOOKS BY MARCUS BACH

They Have Found a Faith

Report to Protestants

Faith and My Friends

Strange Altars

The Will to Believe

The Circle of Faith

God and the Soviets

Major Religions of the World

Adventures in Faith

Strange Sects and Curious Cults

Had You Been Born in Another Faith

Fiction

The Dream Gate

The
Unity
Way of Life

MARCUS BACH

PRENTICE-HALL • ENGLEWOOD CLIFFS, N.J.

Library of Congress Catalog Card No.: 62–18246

Printed in the United States of America
93815–T

Fourth printing...................March, 1963

TO
THE FILLMORE FAMILY
IN RECOGNITION OF THEIR
CONTRIBUTION TO UNITY IN THE
INDIVIDUAL, THE NATION, AND THE WORLD

Contents

The
Unity
Way of Life

The Case for Unity

The Saturday traffic was the heaviest I had ever seen. I had been in it since early morning and now, at midnight, I was part of an endless chain of hypnotic lights and sounds, this time on Missouri highway No. 50. Then I caught sight of a familiar crossing northwest of Lee's Summit at Colborn Road where, not more than fifty feet from the whir of cars and trucks, a sign said: UNITY. Thankfully I drove through the high stone portals, switched my car lights to bright, and as the beam flashed up to touch the quietude of summer shrubbery on either side of a friendly, winding lane, I realized again how close to the world a spiritual retreat can be.

Unity. Officially, the Unity School of Christianity. A spiritual movement without any preoccupation about getting converts. A religious-educational movement teaching the use of God-consciousness in everyday life, clarifying the working of divine law, explaining the action of the mind which it calls the connecting link between God and man.

No one knew how many followers Unity had, and no one seemed to care. People were continually confusing it with Unitarianism, but there was no connection between them. For many years it had no churches and stubbornly insisted that it wanted none. From its beginning, three-quarters of a century ago, it had been an auxiliary type of religion, a booster station amplifying the power of the Christian faith. Here in the heartland of America, some fifteen miles south-east of Kansas City, it has built its imposing headquarters.

Questions and impressions about Unity had occupied me during the long, tiring drive from Chicago. Why, I wondered, was I so often drawn to these grounds both in person and in thought? Religious research, being my vocation, had, of course, included the Unity movement in my field of study, but my interest had gone beyond mere academic investigation. Unity was a new religion as religions go, a thoroughly modern interpretation of the Christian faith. Typically American in its freedom and liberality, it was also distinctly universal in its relationship with other religious groups. Its aim was what its name implied: Unity—unity within the individual as far as the integration of body, mind, and spirit is concerned; unity among classes and creeds as the natural consequence of the brotherhood of man; and unity with the environmental world of nature and of God.

This spirit of Unity pleaded its case as I drove through the peaceful lane to a cement parking lot, one of several on the grounds. It was deserted at this midnight hour, but directly in front of it, like a silent watchman keeping guard over Unity Village, was huge Unity Tower rising two hundred feet into the sombre sky. It was a landmark, known to everyone who had ever walked the grounds, photographed by hundreds of thousands of visitors, and spied by travelers for miles around. Utilitarian in purpose, it was a water tower camouflaged like a campanile, housing an information service with a 24-hour switchboard and a bookstore on its ground floor and offices on the higher levels.

Here, in the shadow of the Tower, with only the whisper of highway traffic stealing in through the landscaped grounds, I thought about a basic concept of mine, one that had been nagging me all day and that had long ago been built into my spiritual habitat: unless religion changes people for the better, it is quite useless. It seemed to me that a man's boast about being saved or not being saved, about his certainty as to salvation, and about being right with God, might actually be symptoms that all is not well with the soul and that a gap still exists between declaration and demonstration in the parallelism of religion and life.

In this connection I had been persuaded long ago that the religion called Unity *had* effected changes in individuals on a remarkably wide scale. Perhaps this was why I had once more come to these grounds, seeking something within myself, but even more, as part of my research, looking for the telltale signs of the changes Unity had wrought in the lives of others.

I recalled my first visit here some thirty years ago. At that time, a Kansas City friend of mine, knowing that I planned to include the Unity movement in my study of religious groups, brought me to this very spot. There were no paved parking lots in those days, no adjoining highways, nothing to indicate that a village would ever rise from these undulating wooded fields. My friend's car bogged down in the mud that day not far from an unpretentious sign that said: UNITY FARM. Disgruntled, my friend predicted that the "cult called Unity" would remain equally bogged down and decidedly short-lived.

He was wrong.

Thirteen hundred acres were developed and from them, by some architectural magic, a settlement was built around a prayer center and a huge printing establishment, the silhouette of which I could see outlined in the shadows beyond the Tower. There were also chapels, cottages, motel units, classrooms, study halls, a cafeteria, a series of exotic fountains, rose gardens, orchards, vineyards, a golf course, a swimming pool, four artificial lakes, and an amphitheatre. Unity Farm became a private Village, incorporated by law, but incorporated even more by faith, the faith that religion can and must change things or it is meaningless.

Unity was founded on that hard, cold fact: either religion

improves your life and your world or it has no real meaning for you. You must find it usable and it must use you, or it has no real significance. Somewhere, somehow, you must demonstrate the power of religion or admit that for you it is powerless.

On these assertions Unity built its case, built it as it had built the Tower, functionally, combining practicality with structure, structure with form, form with beauty, beauty with inspiration. A water tower and a campanile, business offices and a book shop; all symbolized in a monolith, testifying that life, all life, like God and all interpretations of God are one—in Unity.

That is how it seemed to me in these midnight moments when spiritual orientation is an easy and a natural thing, especially at the fountainhead of a faith which insists that one's world is governed by mind action, that no thought is ever lost, and that no encounter is ever without meaning.

Unity was stating its case and my years of research confirmed it: unless there are "fruits of the spirit," of what value are our rites and rituals, and who today is so naive as to believe that a linguistic faith can "save you"? But these fruits of the spirit must be something more than an improved morality or ethical code. There must be a mystical substance in them which goes beyond physical perceptions, which fears no field of spiritual exploration, which shuns no report of "miracles," and ridicules no inner experience no matter how bizarre it may seem. Life, in order to be fully grasped, must be followed in all directions, backward before our physical sojourn began, forward beyond its limiting period in time and space, and inward into what Unity called the awareness of the "indwelling Christ" where the individual discovered his true identity and relationship with God.

This was part of Unity's case. It insisted that true religion has a plus factor which puts it out and beyond the challenge of just being good and doing good or demonstrating a Con-

fucian kind of gentlemanliness. Spiritual evolvement, Unity
believed, is the extension of inner faculties to such a degree
that they are recognized as the Mind of God. When this
discovery takes place, the results so effect the totality of
life and are so startling that they appear to be miracles.
What seems miraculous, however, is but the action of forces
on planes of consciousness not previously understood.

As I sat in my car I imagined that some higher consciousness just then revealed to me two figures moving silently
through the slumbering grounds. I seemed to see them there,
Unity's co-founders: Charles Fillmore and his wife Myrtle.
The former had always been something of a mystery to me,
for he had an uncanny power to heal himself and others.
Having had little formal education, he displayed wisdom
that had always been astonishing. And though he was an
ordinary man to all appearances, as ordinary as a Matthew
or a Simon Peter or any of the others who were called by the
Master in other lands in other days, he had a sense of conviction and purpose far beyond the reach of most religionists.
Because he thought in extraordinary terms about the power
of faith, he was totally unconcerned about those who questioned the nature of his belief. Confident that a cosmic force
was working through him, he was convinced that he would
never die. Part of the mystery was that I believed him and
that I understood what he meant by this remark.

I had vivid recollections of my first meeting with Charles
Fillmore. It took place in the very early years of my research, in the days when I was both eager to believe in
America's new religious leaders and also quick to doubt. A
lurking suspicion that these leaders were not what they
claimed to be was continually struggling against a wish to
believe that they were. More than this, I was always looking
for miracles in those days, confident that when I found them
I would be able to prove that they did not exist. It was in
this contradictory spirit that I first met Charles Fillmore,

and it was because of this that this man of Unity intrigued me at the time.

I had met him at the entrance to the Unity office building when the headquarters were at 917 Tracy Avenue in downtown Kansas City. It was mid-morning, a rainy, misty, autumn morning, but the smallish, energetic man had utter disregard for weather. He was bare-headed, but thrilling, it seemed to me, at the touch of the rain in the wisps of his thin white hair, amused at the sight of his wet hands opening the copper-grilled door as if it were the entrance to some celestial hideaway.

His face was strong but gentle, distinctive from firm jaw to high receding forehead, and the deep-set blue eyes had a way of saying that all was well with the world. I could not have guessed his age, nor did I even think of this. His manner was that of a young man who had just run through the rain, playfully catching the drops in his mouth, flushed with the thrill of nature's response in him. His ears were inordinately large, a fact I recalled particularly because I had the impression he did not really need those ears at all. His art of listening was psychic; he caught vibrations instead of words, and interpreted the articulation of the spirit rather than of the voice. It was with this kind of clairaudience that he listened to the world, and concluded that the case for or against religion had to be judged on the basis of what it did in the individual life.

The record said that he was born in a log cabin near St. Cloud, Minnesota, early on the morning of August 22, 1854, and a horoscopist once pointed out to me that this is a most auspicious time. It is at this conjuncture that Leo, entering Virgo, lifts the sun to the summit of the zodiacal arch. The powerful paw of the lion, holding aloft the sun, becomes a symbol of man's spiritual rebirth. Virgo, the virgin, a woman clothed with the sun, signifies the awakening of spiritual consciousness.

No doubt Charles Fillmore knew all this, for there was no field of metaphysics he had not explored and no area of the occult with which he was unacquainted. For him, however, the deepest consciousness was the indwelling Christ and his metaphysical pursuit was Christ-centered, although every other seer and prophet was invited to come into his life and make his discoveries known. "Papa Charley," as his devoted followers affectionately called him, closed the door on nothing but bigotry. And, speaking of doors, I remember that he left the one on Tracy Avenue open on that murky day, as if to say that if the morning could give no light, he would give what light he had to the morning.

Charles Fillmore's insistence that religion must work, must change people, must demonstrate the power and the presence of God, became the hallmark of Unity and took precedence over any theological or doctrinal device. Self-educated, influenced by the writings of the transcendentalists like Emerson, Alcott, and Lowell, and inspired by the Bible, Shakespeare, and Tennyson, he turned to religion as a quest, to discover for himself what was true about it and what was false.

Like many another man, he was caught in the cross-current of claims by religious leaders who contended that God is this or God is that, that Jesus is to be found here or there, that prayer to be effective must be according to a specific pattern. How, then, was he to find Truth? Like an explorer entering a cave with whatever light he finds ready at hand, Fillmore went into the silence of his inner self to seek whatever there is to be found about the presence of God in the inner life. At a certain hour every night he sat alone, trying to catch a glimpse not of the shadow only, but of the face of God, believing that if God is spirit and if man is also spirit, there must be a line of communication between them or else the entire claim had best be reappraised.

He approached the experiment with as much cold calculation as he did the real estate business which had been his vocation. But gradually something unfolded which led him deeper into the cave than he had ever expected to go, and which gave him a vividly intriguing light upon his way. God, he claimed, came to him during his sleeping hours in dreams, dreams that foreshadowed future events and brought him messages from beyond the region of his conscious mind.

He referred to this guidance as his Monitor and began to depend upon it and act upon it more and more. It became a Presence, a living companion, comparable to the daemon of Socrates, or the light that shone for Jacob Boehme, or the voices that spoke to Joan of Arc. It instructed him to stay in Kansas City. It led him to metaphysicians such as E. B. Weeks, Emma Curtis Hopkins, and to truth teachers such as H. Emilie Cady, D. L. Sullivan, Melinda Cramer and others. It directed him into the spiritual work which was to become his life. It imparted to him out of the silence the name for the work: *Unity*. It endowed him with the power to heal and, with a mind transformed and able, to draw both wisdom and faith out of an infinite, cosmic source. It changed his life and, through him, the lives of others.

At the time of my first meeting with him on Tracy Avenue, he was eighty-three. Had you been there with me, you would not have thought of him in terms of time or years or age. You would have been as unable as I to say he was dressed like this or like that. Just then you would not have noticed that he limped ever so slightly. You would only have known that he was healed, for the story had often been told of how, as a boy, his hip was dislocated in a skating accident and, through wrong diagnosis and mistreatment, the hip socket was destroyed, and he was left with a "withered leg," a leg that stopped growing and which, according to medical authority, would have to be "dragged around on crutches" if the patient lived at all.

Evidently the doctors had not taken God into consideration, as Charles Fillmore decided to do. In all of their years of training, they had not learned what he was to prove, that a withered leg can respond to the power of faith. It responded so remarkably that Charles discarded his crutches, used less and less of a lift to help him in his walking, and eventually his healing became so complete that the limp was no longer noticeable to those who were his associates. So phenomenal was this demonstration that you would almost have understood what he meant when he said that he would live forever, for the medical profession had given him up to die more than sixty years ago!

To be sure, I had the wish to romanticize as well as to challenge the illusions of religion in those beginning years of my research, but now, as I looked back by way of this midnight remembrance, I saw the faith and the power of Charles Fillmore grow tall and commanding as the Tower that loomed nearby. Unity. Unity was his answer to those who insisted that no mystical power exists for modern man and that the fullness of faith belongs only to some ancient dispensation. Unity was his religion, his vision of the world and its people, and, most of all, Unity was his sense of communion with the Presence. Through him, Unity began stating its case in all cultures and countries, saying, "Religion is an experience to be demonstrated. Religion can and must change lives, and through changed lives, the world."

I remembered the stories told about him, some almost legendary in his time, stories that related how, as a very young boy, he was kidnapped by a band of Sioux Indians in Minnesota. They kept him for a day, and it was said that all they did was to bless him in the name of the Great Spirit and then return him unharmed to the log cabin where he lived. Or the lovely story of how once when he was speaking on the subject of Wisdom, an owl came and sat on the window sill throughout the entire presentation.

Then there was the time when a woman came to him and said she needed counsel and advice. Before Papa Charley had a chance to say a word, she went into a long dissertation about her troubles. She never gave him a chance to speak, but after she had exhausted herself and paused for breath, she exclaimed, "Oh, Mr. Fillmore, you have no idea how you have helped me!"

Such remembrances were vivid in my mind as I sat in my car thinking about this man and the great work he started in the American midwest.

He lived in a metaphysical world, but he never lost his connection with the world of men. He talked tenderly about nature and of how the crickets sang, but his inner ear was also tuned to the moods of men. There are memories and reminders of him everywhere on Unity grounds and there are streets in Kansas City which he named: Norton Avenue, named after his brother; Myrtle Avenue, so named in honor of his wife, and streets like Elmwood and Cypress, so named because of his love for trees.

Vivid, too, was my vision of Unity's co-founder, Myrtle Fillmore. Though she passed away in 1931, and although I never met her, I knew her through the reports of a minister friend of mine, a dyed-in-the-wool Evangelical with whom at that time, I enjoyed certain prejudices. We were as typical of the old line churches as the Fillmores were of the new, emerging groups. This particular cleric, no less than I, had been solidly indoctrinated with a bias against "women preachers." It had been made clear to him that the ministry is exclusively a man's domain and under ordinary circumstances he would not have deigned to so much as pass the time of day with a female pastor, much less with a member of a new "sect" like Unity. Fate, however, had maneuvered him into a fateful corner. His wife was a victim of tuberculosis, and he was confronted with the inability of the doctors of his time to cope with the problem. Then by chance, a

Unity publication came into his hands. In it he read Myrtle Fillmore's own testimony of how she had been permanently healed of a tubercular condition through the intervention of the power of God.

So one day my minister friend waited his turn in the Tracy Avenue headquarters. When he was invited into the office where the serenely capable female pastor sat at her letter-covered desk, he said, "Mrs. Fillmore, I am a minister, trained and well-grounded in religion. I did not come here to discuss theology with you because we would not agree. I came to see you because of that story of yours in which you claim you were healed. Were you? And, if so, was it miraculous?"

The regal, silken-haired woman looked at him and smiled. "Would I have written it if it were not true?" she asked. "Do I look like an invalid? Does God want anyone to be an invalid when He has made us in His perfect image?"

"We all have our crosses to bear," continued my friend, seizing on a text which had rarely been challenged and never denied in orthodox circles.

"Crosses are an error in consciousness," was the reply. "They do not exist."

"Oh, come now," my friend retaliated. "My wife is a victim of tuberculosis. There is no error about that. The doctors say—"

"What does God say?"

"Yes, yes, I know," my friend murmured, "but we must face facts."

"Facts are not necessarily truth," the metaphysician corrected. "The truth is that God's healing power is unlimited. It is retarded only by our reluctance to believe and to accept His promises. To realize God, we must believe God. If we are to experience healing, we must affirm health."

With this she went on to tell him that he had surrounded his wife with thoughts of a vengeful God and reminded him that he actually doubted that healing would be possible. She dipped into his mind with such uncanny accuracy that he was completely undone. Then she presented an image of a God so personal, so powerful, and so full of compassion that my friend actually felt he saw his wife, even as the woman minister was saying, "Well and whole, enfolded in God's healing touch!"

It struck him with a shock that this woman with her love and faith had edged in closer to the Lord than he had in all of his seven years of theological regimentation. Of course, she had been trained, too, in education at highly accredited Oberlin College, in metaphysics as a protégé of Emma Curtis Hopkins, founder of the Illinois Metaphysical College, and in faith as a student of Truth.

For a transfigured moment her spirit transported my minister friend beyond the narrow prison of his customary preachments. Suddenly he discovered himself in a world where there were no limiting doctrines, no crosses, and no pretensions about a God of wrath. God was God, a Being clothed with love, less intent on Himself and more solicitous about His children than all the fathers of the Evangelical faith had ever dreamed.

But he soon returned to "reality." The more he tried to analyze whether healing miracles could happen, should happen, had happened, the more he saw again the crosses which, according to his deep-rooted indoctrination, everyone was supposed to bear.

He told me that though his wife was not healed, there was a strange and momentary improvement in her condition shortly after his visit with Myrtle Fillmore. Strange, but not miraculous, was his conclusion. And yet he could never forget the woman preacher who, for a brief moment, had stretched the limitations of his orthodoxy. She remained in his memory, a shadowy and controversial figure of whom it was said that she helped the lame to walk, the blind to see, and the deaf to hear.

She remained in my memory, too, and that is why I seemed to see her on this Unity night, holding to the unyielding creed that every one of us is a child of God, that we are by nature perfect and whole, that we cannot inherit sickness and that we must not accuse a Heavenly Father of vengeance and crosses or anything excepting His love and light shining through our lives.

Filled with these remembrances, I started to walk to the Tower office to check on my motel reservation. It was then that I saw, as I had many times before, one of the greatest secrets of Unity's strength and Unity's growth in the world. It is symbolized by a lighted window on the second floor of the massive main building not far from Unity Tower. This is the window of the room that houses Silent Unity, the lifeline of the Unity movement.

Silent Unity is a perpetual prayer project under the direction of dedicated workers who have one purpose in mind: the channeling of the power of faith directly to persons needing help. You can go to your telephone anytime of the day or night and call Kansas City, LA. 4-3550 and be assured of an immediate and personalized response, instant assurance that prayers will be prayed, and complete confidence that here is no other motive than selfless help through the workability of principles of Truth. Hundreds of thousands of people have memorized that number: LA. 4-3550. Thousands more have written Silent Unity to testify to the power of the affirmative prayers that emanate from this upper room.

There was the wife of a medical doctor in Florida who told me about the miraculous healing of her young son after a tendon in his leg had been so hopelessly severed that it defied surgery. At the age of four the boy wore solid braces up to his hip.

The mother related how the account of the healing of a blind woman through Unity prayers had been a sign to her that God worked wonders even when conditions seemed beyond human hope.

Prayers were begun, with Silent Unity as the hub of a great prayer wheel. The mother was undergirded by these prayers when she kept up her tireless massaging of the boy's limb even when the father, with all his medical skill and faith, despaired that anything could be achieved. But it was achieved and by the time the boy was seven, his braces were discarded and he was healed. A physician examining the final X-ray plates with the first that had been taken, said to the boy's father, "Doctor, if I did not know you I would never believe these are the pictures of your son."

There was a musician in Chicago who was scheduled for a recital, but because he heard that a certain critic would attend, became so frightened he felt he could not go on. He telephoned Silent Unity. "I am playing my first concert tonight. I want to know that you are with me. It must be a success." He was assured that God is the Master of his art. He was assured the recital would be a great success, and it was.

In Iowa lives a young couple whose third child was born deformed. They were told it would very likely be a "crib baby" throughout its life. They heard of Silent Unity and, through its prayers and intercession, were endowed with hope and faith. The child was not healed but the mother said to me, "There is a depth in life we had never found until now. There is a power we have never known until now. There is a new and meaningful world we never discovered until now. God is infinitely good."

There was a university student of mine, a co-ed, whose roommate was in the hospital in preparation for surgery. A call went in to Silent Unity late at night and many of my students who had heard of Unity were interested. The co-ed devoutly accepted Silent Unity's assurance of the goodness of God. She gave praise for health in her roommate's name and there was something about her confidence which, like a spark ignited by her contact with Silent Unity, burst into a flame of faith. She *knew* her friend would not need to undergo the operation and on the following day the doctors confirmed her conviction. They had no explanation. My students did. They said, "If there is anything to religion, why shouldn't things like this happen?"

Early in my research I had checked on the effectiveness of Silent Unity and I had evidence that people's struggles, from sickness to every possible form of tragedy, had been met and conquered. Into the room of the lighted window these calls had come, and not only calls of distress, but also calls of appreciation, praise, and gratitude for problems solved and situations overcome or harmonized. I knew that they were coming now from all over the world, calls and telegrams, more than 1000 every twenty-four hours.

This, then, was the spiritual nerve center of the Unity movement, the sacristy of prayer where God is present in a special way. From this room a mystical force flowed into the most darkened corners of the individual life and lighted that life even as the lighted window cast its glow out on the red-tiled roof and across the grounds where I was standing. To pray is to affirm, says Silent Unity, and for more than sixty years the affirmations have been offered for all who ask for them. They have continued ever since the time that Charles and Myrtle Fillmore met together in their long periods of evening silence, ever since they invited other prayer-inspired people to join them, first in their home, then in a special room on Tracy Avenue, and finally in the new headquarters which were established at Unity Farm in the late 1920's.

Today a hundred and twenty-five dedicated workers, many of them Unity ministerial students, make up the praying staff. They not only pray, they answer each call, each telegram, each request with a personal letter adapted to the specific need. Each letter is blessed. Each envelope is blessed. Each mailing is blessed with the knowledge of the truth that God is Good and that He answers prayer.

I remembered my first visit to the Silent Unity room. I remembered how the sign said simply Silent Unity, but how it seemed to say, "Enter here with good thoughts, for God is Good, and enter in truth, for God Himself is Truth. Come with the Mind of Christ which is perfect love and perfect peace. Come with the image of health in which you were made, and with the spirit of power with which you have been divinely blessed."

There were three connecting rooms, but the one I recalled this night was the one with the perpetually burning light, the votive light of prayer. There was a large round table in the center of that room, divided into arcs and equipped with telephones, and there were workers answering the calls in quiet tones, and I thought I heard them give thanks to those who called that every need is already fulfilled. It was the world of all faiths calling, for ninety per cent of those who ask for help are not Unity affiliated; they are Unity-spirited seekers of truth whatever their creed may be.

I remembered how, when I was in that room, I had picked up a pencil that lay beside a paper pad and how I had closed my eyes to catch in some degree what the Silent Unity workers must experience in bountiful measure—the powerful interpenetration of cosmic thought, the over-whelming awareness of being a channel, an instrument not of oneself, but of God; a feeling that the work is never one's own, or that the thoughts emerge out of self, or that the inspiration is personally induced. No, the creed which adorns the prayer room is the old familiar one, "It is not I, but the Father within me. He doeth the works."

So with closed eyes in the lighted room, I found myself that day writing these words:

> "What is Unity?
> It is the word of Christ made new again,
> The spirit of Christ reborn again;
> The will of Christ revealed again,
> The mind of Christ restored again;
> It is the faith of Christ renewed again,
> The law of Christ affirmed again,
> The love of Christ employed again
> To help man know himself again—
> The Self that is one with God."

With this recollection, I now turned from the lighted window to go to the Tower office to arrange for another stay at Unity Village. The night traffic beyond the grounds seemed far away, as in a world apart, or perhaps it was Unity's world that tended not to shut it out, but, rather, to distill it into part of the totality of life's experience. For Unity's world is one world, the world of living men and memories, the world of hard, cold facts and the secret world with its miracles of Truth, the world of roaring highways and the world of prayer. All are one in Unity, and all are at peace.

CHAPTER TWO

The Unity Viewpoint

A Sunday morning is many things. A time for sleep or a time for play, a time for work or breakfast in bed, a time for the Sunday edition or waking to the sound from a campanile as I did on this Sunday morning at Unity Village.

The song was decidedly orthodox: "The morning light is breaking, the darkness disappears. . . ." It was also a reminder that breakfast would soon be served in the cafeteria and that seven o'clock might be a good time to be getting up.

My motel room was Number One, the first of twenty identical rooms in one long unit. West across a spacious court were twenty more, and east beyond the concrete road were clusters of cozy cottages. These accommodations, within easy walking distance of the main headquarters buildings, were comfortable, quiet and air-conditioned for visitors and people on spiritual retreats. Some of the cottages also served as residences for Unity workers.

In each motel room was a copy of the *Daily Word*, Unity's famous inspirational booklet which since 1924 has popularized the "word for today" idea. Started as a medium for personal meditation, this handsome 50-page 4″ x 6″ booklet has now reached a world readership of millions in 10 languages. Among the many church publications which urge individuals to spend an undisturbed minute with God, *Daily Word* is without doubt the most persuasive and inspiring.

This I realized again when I opened its pages to the reading for this particular Sunday morning. **I Am One with God,** said the caption,

I Am One with God's Light: I Am One with His Life:

I Am One with His Love: I Am One with His Good.

To Be One with Him, I Must Unify Myself with Him in Prayer.

I Must Turn Quietly Within, Where I Can Shut Out All Thought of the Outer World, All That Has Disturbed My Tranquility and Peace.

This was typically Unity. It lost no time in assuring the reader of his consciousness of God. It begged no questions and raised no hints of doubt. It said nothing about the need for penance or self renunciation before God could be approached. It made no reference to inborn sin or evil. It simply and positively affirmed,

As I Feel My Oneness with God in Prayer, He Strengthens My Faith and Fills Me with Courage.

As I Lift My Mind and Heart to Him, I Am Guided and Helped. . . .

I Find the Strength and the Faith to Meet Life Courageously, for I Am Drawing Upon the Mighty, Unlimited Source of Power, of Peace, of Love.

I Am One with God Whose Love Enfolds All Creation.

That was my beginning for a Unity day. A typical beginning for every Unity day because each reading in *Daily Word*, though it differs from the other in content, is quarried out of the same inexhaustible mine of faith and stresses the same indomitable confidence that God is in man and man is in God.

I had read *Daily Word* many times before. I knew hundreds of people who read it: Catholics, Protestants, Jews, Buddhists, Moslems. My first subscription had been given me by a Roman Catholic woman from Ceylon. Whenever I read it I felt surrounded by people of many faiths and cultures who also read it, but at Unity Village this *entente spirituale* took on an even larger dimension.

When I started along the winding road that led from my motel to the cafeteria, I had the feeling that the other visitors who walked the grounds had found their Sunday orientation at the same source as I. They, too, were turning over in their minds the reminder that I AM ONE WITH GOD, and very likely many were asking themselves, as I was, why we so often forget this truth and why we feel alone and adrift in a universe which we know God has made, and which, somehow, He must control and us along with it. Were they as fascinated as I, I wondered, at the thought of how quickly one's attitude toward life changes when we have the courage to recognize this Oneness?

Daily Word had planted the idea that I AM ONE WITH GOD and the Unity grounds were nourishing it, grounds which on this Sunday morning were like a quiet college campus or a place inside protecting walls, though there are no walls and there is nothing monastic about Unity Village. There are no special disciplines invoked here and there is certainly nothing superciliously religious about those who tarry here for spiritual retreats. What Unity is interested in is the discovery of a Spirit, and that Spirit is in you. It says it in many different ways, but the end is the same: I AM ONE WITH GOD.

I have visited the headquarters of many religious movements around the world and they all have their individuality and charm. From Sarnath in India where Buddhism began, to the Holy Land where Christianity was born; from the Vatican, stronghold of Roman Catholicism, to the Protestant fortresses at Wittenberg and Geneva; from the fountain of the Baha'i faith on Mt. Carmel to the gigantic halls of Rissho Kosseikai near Tokyo, Japan, I have seen them all, and in each I felt that in some special way God had imparted a new interpretation of His will.

I felt this at Unity while the music from the campanile continued on this Sunday morning, and while I took a moment to stroll through the exquisite rose garden. Unity believes that a person's surroundings should reflect his thoughts and Unity Village has caught the mood and thought of its believing people.

The red-tiled roofs atop the stately two-story buildings, the immaculately tended hedges in the huge quadrangle, the thousand and more rose bushes, the magnificent elms and maples and rows of ash blending into a warmth of color, augmented my Sunday morning mood. The landscape was an ocean of sensitive shades of green over which the blue and cloudless sky breathed peace. In the series of archways of the Silent Unity building, called The Cloisters, there was nothing hidden or mysterious. Unity had no dark passages, no forbidden doors, no restricted areas. The surroundings, like the faith they represented, were open and free.

It has been said that every new and true religion brings with it a new type of architecture. Do not look for this at Unity, I told myself, for Unity has never professed to be a new religion. Its architecture is a modern application of Italian Renaissance. The buildings are of pre-cast concrete perfectly simulating the sandy hue of weathered stone. The effect is gained by daubs of clay folded into the molding forms and later washed out, leaving the rugged, pitted appearance of quarried stone. The subtle cream coloring is the result of mineral ochers and siennas imported from Italy and deftly mixed into the concrete before casting. This unique construction method was also used in creating balustrades, fountains, urns, and other types of ornamentation. Even the eight-sided dome over the press room was cast in four massive sections and lifted into position by a huge gasoline-powered crane.

Magnificently etched floral designs and figurines adorning the walls of the printery lobby were all made on the grounds. The stenciled designs were cut into the glass by sandblasting equipment. Colored glass mosaics added to the attractiveness of many a pre-cast wall. These mosaics were created by tracing a design on a paper background, then affixing fragments of imported colored glass to the design. Finally the paper with the glass motif was laid in the bottom of the mold and the concrete was spread over it. All of which may still not recommend the buildings as a new type of architecture, but there is one thing this Village does have in its architectural design: unity! The buildings and the landscaping, harmonious as a symphony, represent a sort of spiritual orchestration.

Between the main buildings, a spectacular row of fountains spring from a deep blue mirror pool. This long rectangular "moat" is enclosed by a stone railing, a faithful reproduction of an Ionic baluster. As I walked across the bridge, called, by the way, The Bridge of Faith, I realized again that Unity is not really a village at all, nor is it a movement or a creed or a church; it is a feeling.

It is a feeling that stresses a basic point of view: I AM ONE WITH GOD—AND GOD IS GOOD.

Whether you romanticize religion or whether you are completely cold-blooded about its function in the life of man, on a Sunday morning at Unity you neither want nor need a theology more profound than this: GOD IS GOOD.

Wherever you look, He is good. He is good in the weather, whatever the weather. He is good in the faces of the people, whatever the faces. He is good in the heart of your deepest belief, whatever that belief may be. GOD IS GOOD.

Long ago, in the early days of my research in the whirling

world of faith, I was convinced that all religions have challenged their devotees, aroused their critics, and enshrined
their saints. Each great religion stands before men as a
specific path to spiritual consciousness, to the I-Am-One-
with-God consciousness proclaimed in *Daily Word.*

Among the religions, Zoroastrianism is the path of right-
eousness; Judaism, the path of the law; Hinduism, the path
of identification; Buddhism, the path of deliverance; Con-
fucianism, the path of harmony; Humanism, the path of reason; Islam, the path of submission; Christianity, the path of
love. Unity, a synthesis of all religions, embracing and embraced by all religions, distilled in the essence of Christianity, is essentially the path of goodness. It says, "GOD IS
GOOD" and never ceases saying it.

On this conviction the movement began and on this
declaration it justified its place in the march of modern
faiths. Myrtle Fillmore was healed by the certainty of the
simple but divine idea that she was a child of God and that
because of God's goodness she could not inherit disease.
Charles Fillmore, though he was never completely rid of
physical disability, contended that the goodness of God
makes every thought to the contrary an illusion. In simple
faith he believed that "God made all people good and all
good people nice." Life is good, he kept on assuring himself,
and it is good to share in all the blessings and experiences of
the passing years. Out of this viewpoint came Unity's most
forceful affirmation: There Is but One Presence and One
Power in The Universe, God the Good, Omnipotent!

I caught myself repeating the words, instinctively asking
myself why they seemed so poignant and effective since,
after all, they merely expressed a point of view held by
practically ever religious group everywhere. The only conclusion I could reach was that the Fillmore founders as well
as the followers of Unity not only professed that God is
Good, but practiced it. They did not merely speak the af-

firmation, they lived it. Or tried to live it. They were challenged to follow it all the way, wherever the way may lead. They not only said, "There is but one Presence and one Power in the Universe," they also said, "There is but one Presence and one Power in my *life*," or "in the *world*," or "in my *experiences*," "in my *affairs*," "in my *business*," one Presence and one Power in the Universe, God the Good, Omnipotent!

As I thought about this I stood for a moment motionless and thoughtful in the flower-scented grounds. I said to myself, "How sincerely do *you* believe that there is but one Presence and one Power in the universe?" Set the phrase over against your orthodoxy and your honest conviction and ask yourself what you are going to do with it. Say you have a problem so critical that it simply must turn out as you insist. You pray about it. You put it into God's hands. But it does not turn out as you wish it to. Will you still say that GOD IS GOOD? Will you still truthfully affirm that "There is but one Presence and one Power in my life, God the Good, Omnipotent?"

"Say that you are sick. Say that you have a seemingly incurable disease. What then? Say that something suddenly tragic comes into your life? Then what about the Unity viewpoint that God is Good? Can you as an intelligent and realistic person really subscribe to this philosophy? Can a rational being conscientiously repeat this affirmation in the light of his life from which evil and suffering and sickness and death are never further than a step away? Analyze your life and then honestly decide whether there is but one Presence and one Power, God the Good, Omnipotent!"

Suddenly it was a hazy Sunday morning. Objective creature that I am, I was always trying to see all sides of a question. In spite of my research or perhaps because of it, I shied away from an Absolute like a wild horse shies from glaring light, or, even worse, I was afraid of running blindly into an irrational belief as the same horse would rush into a fire. Just now it seemed to me that Unity was all too uncritical, all too unrealistic in its point of view. It dawned upon me, as it often had in other retreats in other religions and in other countries, that it is easy to lose perspective on the big world when you find a microcosm of quiet and peace. It is easy to feel that hunger and sickness and suffering and inhumanity and injustice and war are mere illusions when you are secure, and when your little world is pleasant and compact. But if God is not *consistently* good, how good is He? Who is to say, "He is good in this instance but not in that?" If we believe He is all good, why do we ever complain or fear or lose hope? On the other hand, what kind of a mind is it which, when we ask of it, "What if God is *not* good?" simply answers, "But He is! How can He be otherwise?" And that was the answer I usually got from Unity followers.

I decided I needed some breakfast. A cup of coffee might help. A man should never wrestle with these problems before his morning cup of coffee, or whatever he drinks. There are religions, like Catholicism for example, in which you partake of no food and enter into no discussion until you have partaken of the Eucharist. And after the Eucharist, you do not feel like arguing. You simply *believe*. Something has been proved to you, though you might not be able to logically explain the process of proof. You walk away from the communion rail with folded hands, *believing*. Like Papa Charley who, with childlike faith never ceased to proclaim that "God is good," you, too, walk away from the Eucharist through a world of your own. Or, rather, through God's world. You walk away and for that moment, no matter what your trial or your struggle or your problem may have been, you know beyond a doubt that *God is Good*.

So thinking, I made my way to the heavily carved walnut doors, the lofty doors which seem more aged than they are, above which a sign said: UNITY INN. I remember telling

myself as I opened those doors that what I really meant was
that God did not seem consistently good to me if my way
became corrupted or confused, or if I prayed and prayed and
no help came, or if my compassion for the world did not
seem matched and far out-matched by Divine compassion.
And something reminded me how I had been praying for
several days in the hope of getting help on a particular
problem, a tough problem, and no help had been forthcoming, certainly no miraculous or Divine help of the kind that
Unity testimonials talked about.

No sooner had I entered the cafeteria than I heard someone call my name. Greeting me was an enthusiastic, young,
outward-going Unity minister who had come to Unity
Village for a conference. He was here among a hundred or
more men and women who were exchanging greetings or
moving through the cafeteria line or finding places at the
long, spacious tables, all in happy moods while a man at
a piano quietly and casually played a hymn, "Safely through
another week, God has brought us on our way!" To the mood
of this song, the minister and I selected our eggs and toast
and carried our trays to one of the polished blue tables.
Here we ate and talked about many things, easy, inconse-
quential things for the most part, but I suppose we both
knew what was going through the other's mind.

The last time I had met this Unity friend was in Florida
when I spoke at his magnificent temple in West Palm Beach,
a church built and served by the effective co-ministry of this
man and his wife. A short week before Mrs. Bach and I had
arrived at their church, this couple had lost their youngest
child, a boy of eighteen months, in a drowning tragedy in
the swimming pool of their new home.

They had left the child in the care of their housekeeper,
a Negro girl in her twenties, while they went about their
church duties. Despite the watchful eyes of the girl, the
child had wandered off and slipped into the pool. When the

frantic housekeeper found him she jumped into the water though she was unable to swim and after futilely trying to rescue the youngster, ran hysterically to a neighbor's home for help.

By the time the parents were notified, the boy had been rushed to the hospital where all efforts to revive him failed. My wife and I had arrived, as I have said, about a week after this had happened. We knew how dearly the boy had been loved and how intense the sorrow of the parents must have been. But we were to learn that in all of our intimate experiences and participation in suffering among the children of men, we had never seen such a demonstration of fortitude and faith as that evidenced by these Unity trained leaders. I was sure I would never forget how, the very next day after the drowning, the father led his three children into the pool and here, standing in the water, they reaffirmed their faith and re-established their confidence that life should hold no fear, that everything is ever in divine order, and that God is good. I have seen evidences of faith before, but such a declaration I had not seen. It was Unity at work at the nerve center of life and to me it was something of a way of wonder.

Our stay with them turned out to be one of our most faith-filled weeks. Now, once more, at the breakfast table in the cafeteria at Unity Village, I recalled the unconquerable confidence of the boy's mother. I remembered that during the moments that the doctors were trying to invoke life back into the tiny body of her son, she was in a hospital waiting-room praying her affirmative prayers. Unity does not implore God. It does not plead with God. It does not even petition God. Unity simply affirms that God's will is done and that that will is good.

That was how this mother prayed, and during her prayer she spied a copy of Unity's *Daily Word*. That a copy should have been in the hospital room is not unusual, but it happened that this was not a current issue, but one that bore the exact month and year of her son's birth. What was more, it contained a poem devoted to the passing of a child and it spoke of God's great love unfolding through the circumstance.

The mother was as impressed by this as if God had placed the copy there with His own hand. As far as she was concerned, He had placed it there. The father of the boy sitting with me at the cafeteria table, said, "Some people would say these things are just coincidental, but when we say that, what have we said? Since everything is in God's hand, isn't that in God's hand, too? Some people ask me how I can bear to look at the pool, remembering all that happened. It wasn't the pool that did it. The pool is what you believe it to be in your consciousness. I look at it as if it were the Biblical pool where an angel came down and stirred the waters, the waters of life, and filled them with healing. I know that I will now be better able to help and heal others who go through similar experiences. If faith does not meet these needs, of what good is faith?"

As we talked, I thought of my strictly orthodox mother, a Christian of the old school, deeply sincere, devoutly committed to the doctrines of the German Reformed Church. I could not help but contrast her attitude about tragedies and death with that of this typical Unity leader. Mother interpreted a drowning or any kind of sudden death as the whiplash of an angered God. We never had a death among our relatives without my mother suggesting that they sell the house and move out. When we had a passing in our family, the rooms were thoroughly fumigated, as much to remove the curse of death as for any hygienic reason, and once, after the premature demise of my only sister, we actually did sell the big house to appease, it seemed to me, the wrath of a chastizing God.

These Unity parents, however, wished only to bless their

home anew, as the minister and the children had blessed the pool. They saw, not the whip of God, but an angel moving on the water. They took what could have been a fateful blow and used it to deepen their conviction that God is good. They had an affirmation: THERE IS BUT ONE PRESENCE AND ONE POWER IN THE UNIVERSE, GOD THE GOOD, OMNIPOTENT.

As I thought about all this on this Sabbath morning here in the cafeteria at Unity Village, I concluded that mortal man has at least two choices: my mother's, which represented the approach of old-time Christianity, or the choice of these young Unity leaders, who typified Unity's insistence that all things work together for good.

They really typified it. They accepted the circumstances surrounding the death of their child as precious fragments which, when pieced together, would be restored once more into the perfect image of God's good will.

It is truly quite a point of view. Evidently when you live and move in this consciousness of God's goodness, there is no doubt as to how far you will go in trusting in Divine omnipotence. You go all the way. You do not say, "I believe up to this point." You never exclaim, "Here I must abandon my faith." Since God's will is sovereign in the universe, you *know* that His will enfolds *everything*. Since He is good, He is *all* good. If you do not fully understand a circumstance or a situation, you nonetheless believe and trust that God never ordains disorder, never sees us as anything less than His creation, and never has any other end in mind than that of causing us in the long run to realize our eternal potential that we are one with Him.

That is what the Unity minister was telling me. He was making it clear that it did not just *happen* that a fellow minister was in Palm Beach in time to conduct the memorial service for his son. It was no *accident* that the distraught housekeeper now found new meaning in religion. It was

not just a *coincidence* that my wife and I came to their home
when we did. All of these occurrences were part of divine
order, evidences of the goodness of God in which there is
always meaning and which is everlastingly alive with purpose.

Purpose. Unity believes that there is always purpose.

Meaning. Unity believes that nothing happens without
meaning.

Divine order. Unity affirms that every intricate detail of
life is bounded by the omnipotence of God.

Unity insists that all life is one and that everything in life
is related to everything else. There is a line, a chain of circumstance, a continuity, and in it all things work together
for good. Unity believes that Chance is God at work, that
a Hunch is the whispering of the Divine, that what men call
Fate is cosmic purpose, and that Coincidence is immutable
law. Live with a horizon that knows no ending! Get the
vastness of infinite vision! Life is an adventure in faith!

What a way to live, if a man has the will to believe!

And how does one develop the will? One way may be to
mingle with Unity people. If you wish to excel in music,
meet and hear the best musicians; if you wish to be an artist,
study the best art; if you wish to learn spiritual techniques,
observe and mingle with those who have employed these
techniques in their lives.

That is how it seemed to me as breakfasters came and went
and as I was surrounded by those who knew me and who
were quite ready to join in the conversation whatever the
topic might be. Unity people are friendly people. You can
recognize them by what I once half seriously called "the
Unity glow." It was my attempt to describe a certain radiance
typical of those who somehow are persuaded in their soul
that God is good, and I say this with no intention of implying
that Unity people are either saintly or beatific or that they
are necessarily better than people in any other faith.

By and large, however, they are individuals who have

found something to live by and who have made the living of it an adventure. They seem to have a good time believing. They give the impression that there are at least two things which a God of goodness is opposed to, self-righteousness and morbidity. They believe in the therapy of the happy heart and in the reminder that what is beautiful is good and that whatever is good is also beautiful.

They represent practically all major religious backgrounds, and it is safe to say that they came to Unity seeking something which their traditional faith had not supplied. Physical healing. Escape from a God of wrath. The need for a positive, hopeful spiritual environment. A search for the common unity of all religions. The challenge of faith in action. Spiritual techniques. No doubt many came as a secret revolt against the institutionalized church which seemingly had lost the personal touch. But most of all, they came because they wanted to believe with all their heart that GOD IS GOOD.

As I listened to the conversation and as I reflected on the minister's attitude about the son he had lost—but did not lose—my problem suddenly seemed of very little consequence and I was about ready to turn it over to God, too, and let it go at that.

Most of us would like to do this, but we lack the courage. We lack the glory of the "foolhardy faith" which, when it has done the best it can, assures us with a certainty beyond doubt that God is somehow working out His will in our behalf. Most of us readily profess that God is Good, but we do not live as though the profession were true. We have the phrase, but not the faith. Most of us pretend that our religion makes us happy, but it doesn't. The majority of us claim that we trust God, but we don't. We have our reservations and our disclaimers and our secret conviction that He cannot quite be trusted, perhaps because of our secret sense of guilt that we have not measured up to this trust.

Thinking through all of this while the breakfasters came

and went and exchanging greetings with Unity students I had met somewhere along the way, I gradually realized that the piano music had stopped, that the campanile was quiet, and that suddenly there was one of those moments when the voices in the cafeteria were hushed and when the whole world seemed suddenly still. My father once told me that these moments usually happened at twenty minutes after the hour or at twenty minutes to. He said it was the time when the angels held their breath. I have no idea where this superstition originated or what this cosmic hiatus is all about, but often during such times I glance at my watch. I did so now. It was twenty minutes to eleven. Breaking the quiet with a laugh, I said, "If a person could just hold on to his childlike faith . . ."

"As for instance?" someone inquired.

"As for instance the feeling that God is consistently good," I said.

To which a woman at the table responded, "But He is consistently good! How could He be otherwise!"

Then the door opened and Lowell Fillmore came into the room, came in without pretense, as he would have to, for there has never been the slightest affectation about this eldest son of the founders of Unity. He would not know how to put on an air or how to appear important, though I suppose you would call him the major-domo of the entire Unity household. Lowell Fillmore, in a very real way, is the co-ordinator of the spiritual and physical functions of the movement, or the general manager or president or administrative director of Unity, but he would be the very last to give himself a title or to be concerned about any such designations. He would rather say that Unity has one director, the Heavenly Father; one general manager, Jesus Christ; and one coordinator, the Holy Spirit. It also has just one principle: GOD IS GOOD. And Lowell Fillmore, in my estimation, is part of that eternal goodness.

"Don't get up, don't get up," he said when I started to rise to greet him, and then added with a chuckle, "The Sabbath was made for rest."

How difficult it would be to find a more guileless or self-effacing man than this well-groomed, white-haired, twinkle-eyed, and soft spoken exponent of all that Unity teaches and believes! He is Unity personified, a selfless, easy-to-meet servant of the cause of Christ as Unity interprets this cause.

I have met many spiritual leaders in my time. I have had to wait for audiences with them in palatial offices. I had to have the right connections and know the right people and present the proper credentials, and be on hand at the right time and place. With Lowell Fillmore it is different. You simply ask, "Where can I find him?" and someone says, "There he is," or "He is at his desk over there. Go and talk to him."

Lowell has dedicated Unity centers all over the western hemisphere. He has written innumerable articles, poems, books, and has carried on a correspondence with the great and the near-great among America's figures in all walks of life. He was at his father's bedside the night Charles Fillmore died. He has spoken to capacity audiences across America, as his father did. Under his quiet supervision Unity has experienced phenomenal years of growth and yet his manner is consistently calm and simple, and he gives the impression that he is nothing more than a Unity worker, which, of course, he is.

That he was born in 1882 in Pueblo, Colorado, is of no particular consequence. No one has ever associated either time or places with Lowell. He is like his father in his wit and homespun trust in God, and like his mother in his certainty and bearing. Among Unity followers whose habits run all the way from food faddists to gourmets, Lowell is the confirmed vegetarian. A man of simple habits, he desires nothing, covets nothing, envies no one, and with his wife, Alice, lives in a world of such remarkable tranquility that others are automatically calmed by his presence. Whatever problems he may ever have had, he carried them lightly. Whatever doubts may have beset him before he formulated his philosophy, he hid them perfectly. Whatever disquietude he may have suffered, he never let anyone see any other token of his faith except that God is Good.

He must have come into the cafeteria by divine appointment, for here was a man I could talk to about my problem. That was my first thought, for I had met Lowell many times before and we knew each other well. Like his father, Lowell always had time, time to visit, time to share. Like his father, he had the gentle capacity for being a good listener, but it dawned on me that in all my talks with him and in all the meetings we had had, there had never been a time when I actually discussed a problem with him. If I was ever tempted to involve him in my personal affairs, he seemed to anticipate it before I spoke and was already assuring me in some oblique way that the solution lay within me because of my own indwelling Christ. I say an "oblique" way because it was done by way of a story or a parable or a reminiscence out of his own experience. They were old stories and old parables for the most part and sometimes I had heard them before. But there was always the absorption of the divine in them, and this was ever new. There was always the feeling that God, being good, already had all the information He needed about my difficulties and that I should rest assured that He would work things out if only I would trust Him and give Him time.

Now, here in the cafeteria, at twenty minutes to eleven, while I tried to bring him around to the fact that perhaps I had a problem of some magnitude, he was talking about a book he had just recently read on the lost continent of Mu. Did I know that the Garden of Eden might possibly have been part of a now sunken island in the mid-Pacific and that Easter Island might be a fragment of a lost continent?

"You've been in Angkor in Cambodia," he said. "Well, you know, the civilization that mysteriously disappeared may be part of the whole great story of how the idea of God traveled from Mu to Angkor to Egypt and all around. Think of the thousands of years and the civilizations that have come and gone, and people are still searching, still searching today. It is really wonderful."

It was even more wonderful, I thought, how quickly he had got me to think in terms of years and forgotten cultures when I felt I had a problem which had to be solved immediately!

You could not help but love the man. He had no opinions or counsel in the sense that these are associated with great consultant or prominent executives. The things that seemed vital to others seemed to him of no particular consequence unless God was first involved in the total picture. And when God was involved, the perplexities were automatically dissolved. Lowell's greatness was the thing he bore within himself, his sense of oneness with all life, his gaiety, his sensitivity, his intellect, his goodness of heart, his love of life. I had no doubt that someday someone would declare that he was a seer.

"What would you say," I asked him point blank, "if a man had a problem and he had been praying and thinking about it and working at it for more than a month and no solution was forthcoming?"

"In a case like that," he said reflectively, "it could be that the man has been trying too hard. There are things we cannot do by ourselves, but when we just turn them over to God, He does them easily."

He looked at me as if to say, "But you probably know that as well as I."

After a moment he said, "By the way, are you going to the service? We can walk over together if you like."

That is what we did. We walked from the cafeteria through the endlessly long printing plant where the giant

presses stood hushed in Sabbath silence, took the elevator to
the fourth floor, and went in to Fellowship Hall where some
six hundred people had gathered for the service.

It was Sunday at Unity Village, and as I sat with Lowell in
the unpretentious surroundings made beautiful by the consciousness that God is good, I thought of a poem that this
quiet man next to me once wrote. Titled, *The Answer*, it said,

> When for a purpose
> I had prayed and prayed and prayed
> Until my words seemed worn and bare
>   With arduous use,
> And I had knocked and asked and
>   Knocked and asked again,
> And all my fervor and persistence
>   Brought no hope,
> I paused to give my weary brain a rest;
>   In that still moment,
> After self had tried and failed,
> There came a glorious vision of God's power,
> And, lo, my prayer was answered in that hour.

Then the service began. The minister asked us to rise and
as we stood with closed eyes, he suggested we join in an
affirmation. He recited it and we repeated it together: *There
is but One Presence and One Power in the Universe, God
the Good, Omnipotent.*

After this we remained for a time in silence, each person
letting the words sink into his consciousness until they became truth, absolute truth, from which there is no willing
escape and in which there is only hope and joy.

We then sat down while the soloist sang *The Lord's
Prayer*, an ever beautiful number which prepared us for the
meditation. These are the moments in Unity when the minister says, "Let us be still and relaxed and let us experience the
presence of God." Then the minister continued, "God always

makes the real decisions in our lives. Until He says 'Go,' don't go. He will make it clear and you will know."

I opened my eyes and looked at the speaker, for it was as if he had read my thoughts. My particular problem had to do with leaving a university post and pulling up the roots of some eighteen years. To me it was a big decision with many overtones and implications and I had been putting it off with characteristic procrastination. I had "prayed and prayed" and now when for a moment "I paused to give my weary brain a rest," the minister's words came as a positive guide. For God had surely never said "Go!" to me in a voice plain enough for me to hear! But now I did seem to hear Him say that I should *not* go and it all seemed right and true to me.

Lowell sat quietly with closed eyes, hands in his lap. What he or others felt, I did not know, but for me just then it was more than the beginning of another Sunday service. It was The Answer. The morning had been more than a reading of *Daily Word* and a meeting with old friends. It was a Eucharist from which one wished to rise with folded hands and, finding his problem mysteriously and wondrously solved, walk with long and lingering steps into a world where God is Good.

CHAPTER THREE

How Unity Worships

A Unity service is so subtle in its simplicity that a newcomer will either be profoundly impressed or completely perplexed, depending on his point of view.

I was convinced of this again as I sat among the worshipers at the service in Unity Village Chapel. Here we were in an ordinary auditorium, a sprawling room filled to overflowing with some six hundred men and women, and having very little to suggest a church-like atmosphere. There was a pulpit in the center of the semi-circular, red-carpeted platform; the organist at the console and the woman soloist were attired in choir robes, but there the formality ended. The minister was in a business suit. Neither altar nor cross adorned this serviceable sanctuary. No candles burned and no statues or stained glass windows suggested anything ecclesiastical. Many a churchman would have argued that "church" was an inept term for these surroundings. But what you *felt* was different, and perhaps true religion is first of all a feeling, at Unity an informal feeling, bringing God down to where man lives and man up to where God resides. And I thought of the saying, "Seeing is believing, but feeling is knowing," and just now I knew I had the feeling.

The secret of a Unity service is in the affirmation, an affirmation carefully, almost delicately placed in a contemplative setting. Go to any Unity church and before the service is five minutes old, you have participated in corporate worship. Something has happened to you. You have professed with your lips and confessed with your heart that you are one with God.

I can never help contrasting this experience with the customary practice in the traditional churches of Protestantism. We open our worship with a processional or a choir number or a congregational hymn. We listen to an invocation or sing the Gloria, or pray the Lord's prayer, but somehow in all this we fail to reach the person in the pew with the thrilling reminder that at this moment God and he are one in a very special encounter.

For participation in worship, Protestantism depends on the hope that the individual will participate. It holds to this hope during the responsive readings or the confession of faith. One would imagine that these would serve the purpose. But they do not. All too often the service remains stereotyped and impersonal. Many of my minister friends complain that their people are apathetic and listless and that sixty percent of their members stay away from the church's services.

There are many reasons and conjectures for this apathy and absenteeism. Perhaps the meaning has gone out of the liturgical symbolism. Perhaps tradition has sapped away the vitality and left the service standing as a matter of form. It could be that Protestantism is no longer sufficiently priestly or no longer sufficiently prophetic, while old religions like Catholicism continue to emphasize the first and the contemporary religions the second. It is apparent that in the historic churches the form is liturgical and the object of worship is God; in Unity the form is non-liturgical and the object is the oneness of God and man. There is never liturgy for the sake of liturgy in Unity or form for the sake of tradition.

I remember the first Unity service I ever attended. It was

a small group meeting one Sunday morning in Kimball Hall in Chicago. I do not remember the minister, but I will never forget how, early in the service, I found myself standing with the congregation, reciting aloud, "THE LOVE OF GOD MANIFESTS THROUGH ME, AND I AM FILLED WITH LIGHT, WISDOM, AND PEACE."

I had been going to church all my life and never once had I been told that the love of God manifests through me! I had stood for prayer in my parental church a thousand times and never once had I testified that, "I am filled with light, wisdom, and peace!" I may have felt all this back in my church environment, but it would have seemed like heresy to have confessed it aloud. In fact, I am not so sure that I did ever feel it without a certain pinch of conscience. God was not this kind of God and worship not this kind of worship. More often than not I was filled not with "light, wisdom, and peace," but with fear, apprehension, and a remembrance of my sins.

Unity affirmations ever after seemed to me like something modern out of Sinai. They dared me to see the best in me and, seeing it, to be my best. They challenged me to come closer to the light and to edge nearer to the heart of God as He passed by.

A man has a right to expect something transcendent when he goes to church. He has the right to be extolled as a child of God. That is what the church is for, that is the true meaning of "church," a special community of special people, and not in any superior sense, but in a sense of the discovery of one's true identity. Here, in the church, absorbed in the awareness of his "true being," a man has at least partially ascended to the top of the holy mount. When he closes his eyes and says, *The love of God manifests through me. I am filled with light, wisdom, and peace,* he arouses these qualities, finds them within himself, in others, and in the world in which he lives.

He hears and knows enough about sin throughout the work-a-day week. He carries on a constant daily struggle with his limitations and there are enough reminders all around him that instead of light he is often in the dark, instead of wisdom he is kept in ignorance, and that in place of peace he is presented with no alternative but war. So he comes to church seeking—and to those who come seeking, it is promised that they shall find.

It is this quality of the quest, incidentally, that distinguishes Unity audiences from most other congregations. I have always found Unity groups easiest to talk to, most attentive in their interest, and most eager for new ideas. They bring a good empathy. They come to a service to learn, to give, to share. They bring a prayer in their heart for the speaker. They are looking for things to live by and for guideposts along the way of truth. Among Unity members the number of those who come to church because they feel they must come is practically nil. There is as yet no traditionalism in Unity which must be perpetuated, no fear of hell or divine retribution which must be appeased, no Sunday spiritual duties which must be kept because it is the thing to do. True Unity people come seeking, endeavoring to see the good, and to improve their life through their recognition of the Christ within.

Their belief or creed, if we wish so to call it, is concise and simple. "There is but one Mind in the universe. Mortal mind is false mind or intellect. It gathers its information from without. Universal Mind sees and speaks from within. Our ways of thinking make our happiness or unhappiness, our success or nonsuccess. We can, by effort, change our ways of thinking. God is at all times, regardless of our so-called sins, trying to pour more good into our lives to make them ever larger and more successful."

One method for pouring "more good into our lives" is done by means of the Word, and by this is meant the posi-

tive, spoken word of faith. The term "Logos" in the sense
that it means the Word of God made flesh in Jesus Christ
may not be any clearer to Unity teachers than it is to traditional theologians, but Unity believes with all its heart that
the actively expressed will of God (Logos) is identifiable
with man.

Worship in Unity means entering into the spirit of worship. Hence, the affirmations. These are not merely words,
they are convictions about God articulated. They are cosmic
forces spun on the vehicle of speech. The mind alone could
transmit them. Prayer could send them from one individual
to another, but in worship they are communicated and expressed audibly to one's true self and then absorbed and
generated in the silence.

Let us imagine that you bring your cares and problems to
the service, as most people do, and as, it seems to me, a man
has the right to do. Did not Jesus say, "Come unto Me, all
ye that labor and are heavy laden," and is not this an injunction that the early church took literally? There was no other
place for Christians to turn, there was no one else to whom
they could go excepting to Him. They saw Him with out-
stretched arms inviting them to "come as you are." The
church today is still an image of that Man in that attitude.
So we come, clanking our chains and dragging our crosses,
and we are given an affirmation, for example, which pro-
claims: I Am Free! I Am Free from All Thought of Worry
and Anxiety, for I Place Myself and My Affairs into God's
Keeping.

There are those who will say that the mere affirming of
freedom does not open prison doors, that the chains are still
there, and the problem has not been overcome. But to those
who believe, to those who fix their minds on faith, every
sense of bondage or burden is lifted when you turn to God
and affirm, "I Am Free! I Am Free from All Thought of

Worry and Anxiety, for I Place Myself and My Affairs into God's Keeping."

There is, as Unity says, and as the Christ promised, release from anxiety and worry when you realize that God is always with you and that you are never alone, that there is nothing too great for Him, that there is no problem that cannot be solved with His help. "Cast thy burden upon the Lord . . . the Truth shall make you free . . . if ye ask anything in My name, that will I do . . ." These and a thousand other texts Unity takes literally.

This is worship—the act of paying divine honor to a Deity by taking Him at His word. This is worship—to honor with extravagant love and extreme submission the Deity's promises. This is worship—to recognize with unflinching courage the truth that since we have been made in the image and likeness of God, we share his nature.

Unity shares it through the Christ. Worship in this sense is essentially an art, and the techniques involved unfold intuitively. The greater the quest, the greater the meaning. What happens in the Unity church service is but a transcript of what happens whenever one worships. Worship represents the "tied to" place, the little world of the spirit.

Unity believes it can be an actual place like a room or a chapel or a grove, an office or a mountain top, or simply a state of consciousness. It can be a vibration to which you attune yourself. What is sought for is that the rate of vibration be in harmony with the deepest experience of the meditation itself. The point of fixation, no doubt, as far as Unity is concerned, is the Christ within.

Who is this Christ? He is God personified. Not a God who can be formed into an image or set upon a wall. Not a God who longs for routine prayers or liturgies rehearsed and dramatized, but a God who works and walks with men because He lives as Man among them.

Who is this Christ? He is the I that I would be. Unity

would say He is the Son of God whose sonship we clearly feel and know when we are with Him in worship. He is the expression of the best in man, the best that man in his upward climb has been able to perceive and in whose perception he perceives himself.

Who is this Christ? He is the Spirit of God incarnate. Not something to explore or to explain or even to examine, but a Spirit to experience by the indwelling light which is the life of every man. He is—and was—a Power and a Presence known and to be known, whose secret source is ever waiting in the secret place of worship.

A Unity service is the extension in depth of this estimate of worship and the Christ. The songs that are sung, rarely more than two or three, more often only one, are affirmative songs, positive in their appraisal of where man stands with God: "Perfect is my heart before Thee, Perfect walk I in Thy ways; Perfect love even now restores me, Perfect is my song of praise."

The sermon, which is the heart and the core of a Unity service, is not a sermon; it is a lesson, and when it ceases to be a lesson and becomes sermonic, it ceases to be Unity. It is an exposition of truth as Unity sees truth, a truth which is at the same time relative and absolute. A truth that has no quarrel with other faiths, that is never in conflict with science, and that is consistently alert to new revelations.

The power of the Unity lesson is in direct ratio to the demonstration of Unity truth in the life of the speaker. The greatest Unity ministers are those who live the greatest lives of faith. This has nothing to do with eloquence, intellectual achievement, or pulpit presence. It is not the word that does the work; it is the spirit within the word.

I know a Unity minister, a woman, whose effective ministry has built one of Unity's largest churches. Thousands come to hear her each week and hundreds have been influenced by the power of her words. She has also had many demonstrations of healing and was herself destined, according to medical diagnosis, to be a paralytic for life. She overcame this through the regimen of faith and, like Charles Fillmore, bore no record of the past excepting a barely noticeable limp.

One day a newcomer to the city came to her for help. The minister counseled this newcomer in her church study and was able to help her with a health problem. When the conference was over and the minister rose to escort the woman to the door, the latter noticed that the minister limped slightly. Thoughtlessly the visitor remarked, "I came to you in the hope that you could effect a cure in me. Now I see that you have not even been able to heal yourself!"

The minister replied, "When Jesus died and rose again he came with a new body, but it still bore the print of the nails. I, too, have risen—from a disease for which I was told there was no hope. My limp is to me but the print of the nails."

This is the spirit behind Unity worship. This is the indomitable persistence that keeps working away at Unity truths.

I know another Unity minister who, together with his wife, has established a work so phenomenal that an orthodox church in the same city once sent a delegation to try to discover the secret of their success. The Protestant leaders could not understand how this young Unity couple with apparently no theological training, no oratorical or pulpit ability, and no traditional background could be so successful. The delegation never learned the secret. It was too simple and too uncatchable. The secret was in their spiritual consciousness. Their success lay in a wonderful truth: we receive in proportion as we use that which we have.

One Unity minister who always fascinated me and who had a following that was highly extraordinary used none of the old techniques that ministers in the historic churches commonly subscribe to. He made no parish calls, he had no use for membership drives. He shunned financial campaigns and carried on no social relationship with the members of his congregation. In fact, there were any number of people on his church roll who scarcely knew him. To analyze his success was impossible for those who did not understand Unity. They knew nothing of his intuitive power or of the fact that he carried his church in his heart. They knew even less of his firm conviction that when the Spirit of truth has come, *It* does the work. Even this minister may never have known what a clear channel he was for the transmission of the spirit of God into the lives of those he blessed and healed and touched in secret through prayer and faith and power in the love of God.

Success in Unity cannot be measured in terms of numbers or in the size of the congregation. The kingdom, as the Scripture states, comes not by observation. Unity has great churches with many members and churches just as great with few members. Often a church is not even the reflection of the minister; it is the lengthened stature of the Unity idea, the idea that every individual is potentially a child of God and that with proper nurture this divine potential can be realized and expressed. This is the power of Unity and this is how Unity worships. Its worship is the surface manifestation of a sub-surface consciousness.

There is a great church on the west coast whose influence has spread like a tide into the lives of people in all walks of life from the movie colony up and down. There is no secret about this work. The minister is a teacher in the true sense of the word, that is, one who draws out from within the individual the unrealized and unlimited power of God's presence. She does not preach, she demonstrates. She does not prepare a sermon exegetically. She is not a theologian's theologian. She is something more, a messenger of truth as she sees it and a courageous purveyor of that truth.

The story is told that when this minister decided to leave

the doors of her prayer chapel open day and night, the police warned her against such a foolhardy innovation. They were sure this would be an invitation to vandalism. They knew from their experience that you cannot trust people that far. But the minister had her own experience. She said, "God is standing at the door and He will take care of things." God did take care of things, even to allowing a drunk to come in and sleep in one of the pews one night.

The degree of this type of faith varies as the leaders vary, but the worship of Unity is the worship of a Power which the world has all but rejected, a mystical power which is responsive to faith. The deeper the faith, the deeper the power. The deeper the power, the deeper the worship. The deeper the worship, the more glorious the life.

Many are the new Unity churches I have visited, beautiful, inspiring churches, and many are the times I have walked with the minister through his church and heard him say, "None of this is my work. All is God's. It sort of happened around me." "Through me," might have been more correct, for that is how God works in Unity. That is how He works in worship. God is the light and what He wants, evidently, are leaders whom the light shines through. Do not struggle, do not strain, do not even seek—just accept, such is the watchword and the technique. For the orthodox mind it is all too simple and, therefore, incomprehensible.

I have sat in many Unity churches and heard the people repeat the affirmation, "Unity is *Growing, Growing, Growing!*" and as they said it you could feel the growth. You could see the churches rising from small groups of believers to great congregations of doers. They bore the Unity name: Unity at the Crossroads of the World (New York City); Unity by the Sea; Unity of the Palm Beaches; Unity Christ Church; Unity Church of Christ; Christ Church Unity; Unity Center of Truth; Unity Truth Center; Unity Church of the Valley; Unity Church of the Oaks; Lakeside

Unity; Unity of Miami, of Chicago, of Cleveland, of Oklahoma City, of Detroit, of Escondido, of Des Moines, of Milwaukee, of New Orleans, or Boston, of your hometown and mine.

And all the people said, *"Unity is Growing, Growing, Growing!"* and Unity grew.

How does one become a Unity member? Actually there are no specific acts or requirements. Some centers do not even have "members" although people may apply that designation to themselves if they wish. Each church sets up its own requirements, and about the only thing they all hold in common is the lovely and simple policy that Charles Fillmore followed throughout his long and eventful life. "I talk and think to God," he said, "and God talks and thinks to me."

What do Unity members talk and think about—to God? Everything.

I have been at Unity services where prayers or affirmations have been directed toward the weather; the weather which is something that scientists are just now beginning to try to do something about. It is also something that animistic groups have tried, sometimes with success, to regulate through abracadabras or occultism of a type beyond our knowing. Unity is not afraid to look both ways, to ancient animism and to modern science.

I heard a Unity prayer during a time of drought that went like this, "Divine love blesses the earth with perfect weather and the proper amount of moisture. Order, harmony, and safe conditions are established." We repeated this affirmation en masse and then stood in silence, almost, it seemed to me, as if listening for the first drops of rain. They did not come during the service and, since I never checked back on the record, I do not know whether they ever came. But I do know that in the minds of the worshipers God's will and God's order *were* established, and I have no doubt that when man has once learned the complete harmony between his mind and God's mind, divine love *will* bless the earth, and order and harmony *will* be established.

Furthermore, this Unity outlook is one to which I can testify when I remember twenty trees that I planted on my cabin hill in British Columbia. A dry spell took a toll of ten of these seedlings despite everything I could do to save them. A visitor observed, "Half of your trees are dead." I caught myself saying, "The way I see it, half of my trees are living." It was a matter of the point of view. Mine was Unity's.

Worship ought by rights to be a factor in the development of a usable approach to life. We should come away from a service with our spiritual batteries charged with Good, our outlook on life changed for the better, our slumbering awareness of God's spirit aroused. We should be different creatures when we come out of a service than when we went in, and no matter how spiritually inclined we were when the service began, we should be even more spiritually motivated when it ends.

Many Protestants have confessed to me that when they go to services in their parental churches they feel like sinners. They are critical of the minister, they have difficulty believing what he says, they are disenfranchized with the order of service, they feel a semantic gap between what they hear and what they interpret. This is not true in Unity where every sermon is a lesson in truth and where you are always given at least one thought or one technique which has a practical bearing upon your life.

I remember the Unity family who confided to me that their home used to be divided because of their religious differences. The husband was a Protestant, the wife a Catholic, the two children were being brought up in the Roman Catholic faith.

"We used to go to our separate churches," the young wife

said, "and we used to quarrel all the way home. Since we have come to Unity, we go home singing."

There is another thing. Whenever I see an offering taken at a Unity worship service, I recall my days in the active ministry of my parental church. Money, in more ways than one, had always been one of my greatest embarrassments! I could never quite reconcile the two, money and religion. I had been taught that one was Caesar's and the other was the Lord's; one was Mammon and the other God, and somewhere in my thinking the two were irreconcilable since time began.

I remember the collection plates all the way from my boyhood when, in my uncle's church, the long-handled, deep, black-pocketed *klingbeutels* were defiantly passed along the pews until the worshiper felt he had a bayonet aimed at his heart, or, better, at his hip pocket. I stressed tithing in one of my churches, but it did not work. I suppose it did not work because I myself was not tithing. Evangelists in those days had other approaches. Aimie Semple frequently strung a clothes line above the pews and ordered the worshipers to pin their offering on it. Billy Sunday worked people into such an emotional pitch they automatically emptied their pockets. Wilbur Voliva introduced the offertory march during which the congregation dropped their money into huge barrels to the blare of a big brass band. Still today, in most churches, the offering is a rude break in an otherwise sanctimonious ritual.

In Unity the offering is plainly and simply a part of worship. It is done with a most excellent decor. You press your offering in your hand and bless it. It is no longer filthy lucre or Caesar's gold or Mammon's petty cash; it is part of the Kingdom's business and an expression of God's love and bounty.

The minister explains, "We have a custom in Unity to bless the offering by holding it in our hand and joining in an affirmation, 'Divine love, through me, blesses and multiplies all that I give and all that I receive.' Let us now close our eyes and repeat these words together."

Once more the simplicity is so subtle that it may perplex the newcomer to Unity. He feels something quite inexplicable within himself as he speaks the words, and for once the customary "collection" takes on the semblance of a sacred act. Just why this is so is not quite clear unless it can be explained by the simple fact that there is power in the word.

Many Unity members tithe, giving a tenth or more of their gross or their net income, depending upon the degree of their faith. There is very little talk about money in Unity, very few campaigns or "every member canvasses" or drives to raise funds. Charles Fillmore put the matter into plain and practical terms. When it comes to giving, he said, there must first of all be a willing mind. Secondly, the giving must be done in faith, and with no withholding just because the offering may seem small. Thirdly, the offering should be a just and fair proportion of all that one receives.

"True spiritual giving," he explained, "rewards with a double joy. First that which comes with the placing of the gift upon the altar of the Lord; secondly, the joy of sharing our part of God's bounty with others. One of the blessings is the satisfying knowledge that we are meeting the law and paying our debt of love and justice to the Lord. Justice comes first, then generosity."

Of course, there is no guarantee that the advice of the founder of Unity will always be maintained either in the economy or in the polity of the Unity movement. Whenever I attend Unity church services across America, when I see the building programs and the astonishing growth of this faith, I remember that it was Charles Fillmore's hope that the work should never develop into another denomination. The movement, as far as he was concerned, was to be restricted to a training center, a school in which people of all communions might share their experiences, deepen their faith, and re-examine their convictions in the light of the full promise of the gospel of Christ.

This is what made Unity distinctive and unique in the days of its youth. It sought no converts. It launched no missionary activity. It wanted nothing for itself except the fellowship of students of truth, students who would return to their churches strengthened and inspired. It may be that Charles and Myrtle Fillmore were highly unrealistic in this approach. They should have known (perhaps they did know) that never in the history of religions has a new movement failed to take on an institutionalized form. Even the various movements within Catholicism are no exception, and the many "sects" within Protestantism are proof that when people begin to believe alike they are bound to band together and become church-like.

History may not always repeat itself, but its pattern remains constant. There is no reason to believe that the Unity School of Christianity will not one day be rated as a denomination. The pattern is already becoming apparent. Some eighty years young, it is already a church of striking proportions.

In all religions there is always first the unbounded passion of the founders, then the years of growth, then the leveling out in which the passion passes over into a theology. The one factor that may save Unity from going the way of other movements is that it recognizes this pattern and is doing something about it. It knows that the history of religions is a four-act drama. The first act is like the spring when the movement is born because of the power and, as has been said, the passion of those who had the original experience. In the summer, act two, the full flowering of the seed evolves among its ardent devotees. In the autumn, act three, the movement becomes institutionalized, and in the winter, act four, it loses its vitality.

Unity knows this. It recognizes that it now stands in late summer, in the closing moments of the second act. Its hope lies in its confidence that the old dramaturgy is not immutable. It does not subscribe to the superstition that there is no other script or that the scenes cannot be changed. In a very real sense it insists that the zeal and experience of its founders can and are being reborn within the lives of its contemporary leaders. To the degree in which this is true, Unity can mold its own destiny and dictate its own tomorrow.

The heart of the matter lies in its worship. It is worship that reflects the depth of the minister's experience. It is worship that gives the people an insight into the quality and degree of their own spiritual consciousness. It is worship that mirrors the inner life of leader and people. Worship *is* a feeling, an empathy, a response, which every worshiper registers and takes home with him and lives with and thinks about in the silence of his deepest contemplation. Unity worships by way of demonstration which means that there must be tangible evidence that God is at work or else the work is not of God.

Traditional denominations living in the autumn or winter of their history have other criteria. They count their success in numbers of converts, in numbers of churches built, in numbers of schools established, in social influence, or in their political impact. With Unity it is not so. It has only one criterion: the realization of the indwelling Christ in each worshipper.

I have frequently criticized Unity for its lack of missionary activity, its failure to develop a deeper theological base, its apparent unconcern for some of the global issues of our time. I have questioned its depth and have wondered about its Christology as well as its syncretic approach. But whenever I share in Unity worship, I am persuaded that Unity is right in putting first things first as it sees them. Which is by way of saying that until the individual is changed, it is futile to try to change the world and until the simple rudiments of the Christ are understood, theology has no way of changing the man in the pew or, for that matter, the minister himself.

Unity worship says in effect that one should not expect religion to effect peace in the world until it has brought peace to one's own life. It cannot solve problems between nations until it has solved the personal problems that beset *you*. It cannot inspire universal love until it has taught you the meaning of love in your own life.

The world gets better only as people get better. If one man could do it alone, then the beginning of the Christian era or the years of the life of Christ would have been years of peace and brotherhood and love.

But they were not.

The times of the historical Jesus were also the times of the Caesars, of Augustus, a Varus and a Titus. Until love and faith are born anew in enough individuals to outweigh those who persist in advocating hatred and fear, it is futile to look for a new heaven and a new earth.

The challenge is personal and, therefore, Unity is above all a personalized faith.

Unity worship emphasizes the fact that this personalization, this applied Christianity, as it calls it, is a distinctive which Jesus enunciated when He said, "If you love them which love you, what reward have ye? Do not even the publicans the same? And if ye salute your brethren only what do ye more than others?" In a very real way Unity is the gospel of the second mile and worship is a guideline along the way.

Unity worship closes with a blessing, a benediction, or, not infrequently, with the Unity prayer of protection. It is a beautiful prayer and all Unity people know it, love it, and use it. They repeat it around the world wherever Unity people gather. You can hear it in Germany where Unity work is just beginning, and in Japan where ministers have just recently gone. You can hear it in Nigeria where Unity affirmations are accompanied by the beating of native drums. You can hear it in Great Britain where centers are being opened with an almost revivalistic passion. I heard it as the service closed in Unity Village Chapel:

> The light of God surrounds you;
> The love of God infolds you;
> The power of God protects you;
> The presence of God watches over you.
> Wherever you are, God is!

And hearing it, I had the impression that Unity people mean it and believe it. Which they do.

CHAPTER FOUR

How Unity Works

Every Monday morning at eight o'clock another week begins at Unity Village. The workers come in cars from their "off campus" homes or on foot from nearby cottages. Seven hundred men and women open the doors of another day in one of the world's most unique religious centers.

Some of the workers patronize the cafeteria for a seven-thirty breakfast with the chance for a brief visit or an occasional impromptu song if the spirit dictates. They do not start work at eight. They "stir up the spirit of Unity" in a thirty minute meditative session. Assembling in Unity Village Chapel, they are welcomed by a Unity Minister or a ministerial student, listen to a solo or a duet, and then give attention to a "lesson" by Lowell Fillmore who, for nearly twenty years, has been guiding the Unity family in this matin hour.

No one could present the lesson with more sincerity than Lowell. No one could project the simple faith and subtle power of Unity teaching with more quiet authority than does this eldest son of the founders of the movement. His remarks deal with the application of the Christ consciousness in modern life, especially as it pertains to the day at hand. To Lowell, every day is a series of God's moments, generously woven on a cord of truth and faith.

While there is nothing compulsory about this Monday

get-together and even though less than twenty percent of the employees are Unity members, a tradition has been established and the workers turn out en masse. So successful are these services that they are now held several mornings throughout the week, but Monday is the established time and Monday is Lowell Fillmore's morning.

Industry and business could learn something from these meetings, for here one's sights are lifted above the mere mechanism of a job. Here is a moral and spiritual inspiration bound to induce better work and better group relationships. The session on this morning at this "Workers' Chapel" closed with its customary affirmation: "Our words are spirit and they are life, and they do accomplish that whereto they are sent." This, I thought, was a most appropriate statement for any publishing enterprise!

That is how Unity works.

I visited some of the departments to discover for myself the total impact of the Monday morning meeting, wondering how Unity philosophy actually worked in the day-by-day routine. This was a good question, it seemed to me, for I have met many people who *talk* a good way of life but who have a hard time living up to it. I know therapists who, though they write impressively, desperately need therapy themselves. I have met ostensible spiritual leaders who bemoan the fact that they preach a much better type of religion than they practice, and because of personal experience I appreciated their plight. When you "get religion" even your dog or cat should see a change in you. So naturally I was interested in discovering what effect, if any, Unity teaching had on people in Unity jobs, especially after they had begun a new week with a half hour of spiritual indoctrination.

I went first to the mail department, a large, efficient room in the administration building. Now I should think that the handling and opening of mail could be a most monotonous chore, even though there may be contributions tucked away in many of the envelopes. This morning there were nearly 10,000 letters. That is a lot of mail, but, then, Monday morning is heaviest. During the remainder of the week there will be a daily income of 6,000 to 8,000 letters. That still is a lot of mail.

No sooner had the truck rolled in with this cargo from the Lee's Summit post office and no sooner had the bulging bags been emptied than the "Mail Opening" workers, some thirty in number, gathered in a circle to bless the letters. This, in itself, was an innovation. In how many businesses, even religious businesses, do you suppose this happens? Who blesses a letter before opening it? It happens at Unity every day because Unity is a prayer project from top to bottom and if it ever ceases to be just that it will cease to be Unity.

The mail-blessing, led by Kenneth Jarman, went as follows, "We are a channel for the blessings of spirit upon these letters and we manifest order, accuracy, and promptness in our work."

After this impressive statement the letters were sorted according to the various departments, then transferred to the desks where the money, checks, and subscription lists, inquiries, book orders, and comments were carefully processed. It was clear to me that the inspiration of the morning session had definitely left an impression. A spirit of cooperation could be clearly felt, and the emphasis that work is worship had reduced friction to a minimum. Many times as the mail goes to its various departmental destinations, it is blessed again and when answers to correspondence go out through the letter-writing offices a final prayer is put upon them which affirms, "The Christ consciousness of peace, power, and plenty is expressed in this outgoing mail."

Observing this, I thought what a good idea it would be for every business to handle its correspondence in this fashion. In most offices the mail is torn open or slashed with a paper knife in a manner so impersonal that the sender might well cringe under the impact. In Unity, where thoughts are things, it is believed that the attitude in which mail is received and handled is telepathically transmitted to the sender. Unity would not call it telepathy. It would very likely refer to it as the wings of thought. Unity's symbol, incidentally, is a pair of wings which, in all ages and in all religions, has been a sign of transcendency. It has long been a belief among metaphysicians that the gossamer wings of thought carry impressons straight to the source which inspired the contact.

So letters are treated with courtesy and respect, and a literal chain of prayer carries them to their prescribed destination.

Does a letter contain a complaint? Unity tries to discover whether or not it is justified. Does a correspondent offer suggestions? Unity sincerely considers them in the light of impartial understanding. I saw a letter which accused the department of neglecting to fill a subscription. The writer insisted that the money had been sent on a certain date but that the periodical had not been received. When I asked what would be done about this, I was told that the subscription would be entered immediately and the literature would be sent without question. Rarely, if ever, is the writer challenged. Here at Unity the subscriber is always right. More than once, letters arrive later saying, "After writing you about not receiving my order, I found that I had not mailed my subscription. Thank you for sending the order just the same. Check is enclosed."

On several occasions sacks of mail have been unintentionally mishandled at railroad stations. It seems that mail trains picking up the bags on the fly sometimes travel so fast that the platform mechanism catapults the sacks under the grinding wheels where they are torn to shreds, sucked up under the train, and carried for great distances. Unity has received shreds of such letters after these were found in farmers' fields and along the railroad right of way. In every case the scraps were reassembled and the letters acknowledged. Once, part of a $36 check was found in a wayside ditch. Then other tattered shreds were found and returned to Unity where they were pieced together until the check was again intact. Unity looks upon all such occurrences as evidences of the working of divine order.

Divine order governs all departments throughout the vast Unity structure, a structure which is not easy to separate into specific categories. The activities in this vast movement are overlapping and the personnel is involved in a total rather than a departmental plan of operation. However, I see Unity as a fourfold organization consisting of:

1. The Publishing Department
2. The Department of Spiritual Service
3. The Department of Educational Training
4. The Farm

Publishing is in itself, of course, a form of spiritual service, for in Unity the WORD is life. But as far as operational function is concerned, the printing is big business, nonprofit business to be sure, but big. Unity produces 50 million pieces of printed material annually, including 18 million magazines. More than a million people read Unity periodicals, titles of which are *Wee Wisdom* for children, *Progress* and Unity Sunday School Leaflet for teenagers, *Weekly Unity, Unity, Good Business,* and *Daily Word* for young and old.

Daily Word is, of course, the most popular. It is published in ten languages besides English: Afrikans, Dutch, Finnish, French, German, Gujarati, Japanese, Portuguese, Sinhala, and Spanish. The Spanish edition, *La Palabra Diaria,* is printed at Unity headquarters, the Portuguese is brought out in Brazil, and the others are published in the country

where the language is spoken. There are 174 countries on
Unity's global list.

Five publications are printed in Braille and distributed
free to the blind: *Daily Word, Progress, Wee Wisdom, Lessons in Truth,* and *Finding the Christ.* The latter two are
books.

Unity publishes more than fifty books, including a Bible
dictionary, histories of Unity and its founders, a vegetarian
cookbook, inspirational and metaphysical books, a songbook,
children's books, and pamphlets and tracts. The sales of
books and magazines cannot begin to cover the huge printing cost or meet the expense of Unity's benevolent services.
Every month, tens of thousands of magazines, books, and
other literature are distributed free of charge to charitable
institutions, religious groups, and needy individuals. Therefore, the work is financed mostly by love offerings sent in by
friends.

That is how Unity works.

If *Daily Word* is most popular in the publishing department, then Silent Unity is the most eminent in what I have
called the Department of Spiritual Service, the second
classification in our attempt to define the Unity structure.
When I walked through the long halls where the presses
turned and where the colorful pages of the magazines flowed
along the assembling and stapling tracks, I had the feeling
that the world was reaching in, wanting to be filled with
thoughts of hope. When I walked into Silent Unity, where
the only sound was tranquility, I had the feeling that Unity
was reaching out, filling waiting hearts with prayer. As the
printed word goes forth from the presses, so the spoken
word goes out from the room of the lighted window.

The Silent Unity rooms are sacred. The silence is sacred.
The prayer sanctuary is sacred. Here where 150 faithful
workers of Silent Unity pray in relays of 6 to 8 day and
night, I had the same response as when I visited other great

spiritual centers: rooms in the Vatican, chambers in a Mormon Temple, sacristies in great cathedrals, meditation rooms in Buddhist temples, sanctuaries in famous churches, prayer rooms at shrines where miracles have taken place.

I agreed with Unity when it says, "From Silent Unity goes the spoken word of Truth which carries healing, comfort, and happiness to millions throughout the world." People turn to Silent Unity for help in solving every conceivable problem. Not only do they request prayers for healing, but also for prosperity, employment, protection, better grades in school, freedom from undesirable habits, the adjustment of misunderstandings, and the solution of domestic and various other problems.

Those who write to Silent Unity are helped and blessed by the awareness that the power within themselves—the power of God—is being released. A latent spiritual force is released because the request is already a key, a key that unlocks this hidden power. The workers not only pray, they write to those requesting prayer or speak to them over the telephone. But most of all they "stir up the spirit" through affirmations, faith, and consecrated lives.

I visited with May Rowland, director of Silent Unity, in the consultation room built originally for Charles Fillmore. The tranquility here left no doubt in my mind that God dwells most surely in the calm. The quiet surroundings, the simple, stately chairs, table, and hearth are right for this setting, and May Rowland is right for Silent Unity. Through more than half a century of service May is a symbol of the inner calm, a fine example of those who have learned to still certain senses, to hush certain impulses, to enfold in a mystic kind of serenity the circumstances which so easily toss most of us about.

There will be legends about May Rowland in the long years ahead and most of them will be true. As Unity builds up its history, May's books will be read as classical Unity

studies, her recordings will be played, and her lessons will
be remembered as examples of what truth lessons should be
like. I already believe some of these legends as, for example,
the time when May stood on the verandah of her home on
the ridge near Unity Village and affirmed that the black,
funnel cloud of a tornado, ferociously dipping to the earth,
should bypass Unity, which it did. I believe the testimonials
of the people who have told me what May's prayers have
achieved in "healing miracles," what her words have ac-
complished in helping the helpless, and what her life has
done in inspiring those who desperately needed guidance
along their way. In the serious business of life and in dealing
with those who have walked the edge of tragedy, May has
never lost either her sense of quiet humor or her remarkable
poise—but, then, that is how Unity works.

And it occurred to me that if I were to select one practice
out of the many which Unity has proclaimed, it would be
the "secret of the secret place." Whether it is Silent Unity
or merely the silent heart of every believer, this is where the
changed life is wrought: in the meditative retreat from the
world.

Every Unity minister and every sincere student of truth
knows that the life lived in the open is but a surface reflection of the life lived in closed sessions with the Spirit.
Charles and Myrtle Fillmore taught and demonstrated the
need for this kind of meditation. The secret of Unity's
growth and appeal is localized at this very spot: the secret
of the secret place.

Religion, any kind of religion, can effect little change in
the individual unless he is willing to do his own inner research in the laboratory of his life. This is the "home work"
without which the whole religious process is rather meaningless. The reason we find so little difference between church
members and non-church members throughout the world is
because mere church affiliation has no more significance

than affiliation with any fraternal organization unless the individual embarks on his own spiritual quest and puts a period of meditation at the heart of it.

This Unity seeks to do. It is geared to this ideal, an ideal which is referred to again and again as the "awakening within of the incarnated Christ."

That is how Unity works. I realized another extension of this when I visited, as I had often done before, the work of Silent-70. Not to be confused with Silent Unity, Silent-70 is nonetheless an integral part of what I have called the Department of Spiritual Service. It is usually referred to as the missionary arm of the Unity movement. It sends out not people, but the Word, sends it out in many forms: books, pamphlets, prayer cards, tracts and magazines, distributed without cost to hospitals, homes for the aged, orphanages, social welfare groups, military organizations and penal institutions.

Begun in 1890 by Charles and Myrtle, Silent-70 is an application of the 10th chapter of St. Luke's gospel, "The Lord appointed other seventy and sent them . . . into every city and place . . . and he said unto them, The harvest indeed is plenteous, but the laborers are few."

Unity was not interested in competing with the churches nor was it anxious to attain an institutionalized status. It wanted only to disseminate truth and apply it to modern life. It had a compulsion to get this word to groups which, even today, are all too often forgotten, particularly those in hospitals and prisons. Key people were therefore assigned to the distribution of Unity literature wherever the need for such material was established and, working in cooperation with chaplains—Protestant and Catholic alike—they made their contribution in a unique and specific way.

I talked to Nina Wright, director of Silent-70, about the prison work, for I doubt whether there is any other spiritual agency in America which has done more for prisoners than has Silent-70, and few have been more dedicated to the job than Nina through her more than thirty years of service. She personally conducts monthly meetings in prisons, but this is merely incidental to the nationwide program which Silent-70 has developed through the years.

It is a fantastic program, one phase of which is made possible through the cooperation of a nationally-known greeting card company. This firm turns over to Silent-70 literally truckloads of expensive cards commemorating holidays and special occasions. These cards represent designs which have been currently changed, lines which have been discontinued, and stock that has been over-produced. Some of the cards originally sold for as high as a dollar or more, but now they are turned over without cost for free distribution to prisons through Silent-70.

At Christmas time or Easter, as well as other holidays, prison inmates may request through their warden or chaplain as many of these greeting cards as they may need for mailing to friends on the outside. Silent-70 sends them both cards and envelopes, sends them by the ton to the world of forgotten men. Many are the lives that have been touched and changed through this unusual service.

Lives have also been transformed through Silent-70's distribution of literature and correspondence courses in religious truth. The testimonials are overwhelming.

"Dear Silent–70," writes a prisoner from the penitentiary at Fort Madison, Iowa, "What an inspiration I receive each morning when I reach for the *Daily Word*. Not as a crutch but as something I have placed faith, hope, and belief in. I pray others in prison and outside share my feeling. There is such a deep need by each of us in prison to believe in something and someone. Your work for God has and will continue to help so many."

From Alcatraz to Sing Sing the influence of Unity has gone and rarely does a prisoner forget the impact it has made. Many write to Unity headquarters after the prison doors have opened. One letter, typical of many, came to my attention in the Silent-70 files:

"Will you please accept the enclosed thanks offering and use it in your wonderful work of providing truth literature for inmates of institutions?

"Nineteen years ago I spent my first Christmas away from loved ones and for days my spirits were at a hopeless, discouraged, low ebb. I was serving a sentence for embezzlement. The fact that I had been guilty of the offense and that my sentence was a just one did not dispel the self-pity, the worry over the welfare of my wife and children at home, nor the terrible loneliness that oppressed me.

"Then one day in the prison library I picked up a copy of *Weekly Unity*. Today I do not remember the name of the article but I do remember the affirmation that it contained. It was a light in the darkness for me and I memorized it by constant repetition. It was: LOVINGLY I PLACE MYSELF, MY LOVED ONES, AND ALL OF MY AFFAIRS IN THE FATHER'S HANDS AND I KNOW THAT ALL IS WELL.

"Gradually as I repeated the affirmation in desperation came the faith that it was true. Then things began to happen. A letter from my wife told of a position she had obtained that assured the well-being of her and the children. Next, I was given a job behind the walls that kept me busy and gave me a measure of contentment and peace of mind.

"Life has changed since those dark days. I completed my term and returned to the small town from which I went to prison. The hometown folks have been kind. They have accepted me as one of themselves in spite of my mistake. . . . God is good to me and I am thankful. I am also thankful to you whose ministry brought to my attention an enlightenment that was so sorely needed."

Sometimes chaplains add a humorous touch, as in the letter from Chaplain Father Eusebius of the Penitentiary of New Mexico.

"When I announced to the men that Christmas greeting cards would be given to them to send home and that the VFW would take care of the stamps and the mailing, some said, 'What's the hitch there, Padre?' and 'Sounds kinda fishy to me.' and 'Why you being so good to a bunch of damn cons?' Then I began making explanations and here is the title they gave to you (Nina Wright) 'She must be the sweetheart of all the cons.' I will indeed remember you in my prayers and all other religious exercises and activities."

The third department, the Department of Educational Training, means many things. It means, first of all, the training of truth students, not ministers only, but teachers, center helpers, and individuals who make up the Unity rank and file.

For all of these there is a Unity Correspondence School Course with a basic text, *Lessons in Truth,* by H. Emilie Cady. The course consists of two units of six and twelve lessons respectively with a curriculum including such subjects as "The True Character of God," "The Body of Christ," "The Formative Power of Thought," "Denials and Affirmations," and "Judgment and Justice." There are also introductory courses in Unity fundamentals and postgraduate courses in advanced studies in truth.

"How does one become a Unity minister?" I asked Lowell Fillmore.

With customary simplicity, he answered, "One comes to Unity headquarters for study and for work in Silent Unity. The principal method consists of a three-year course, courses in practicing the presence of God, in prayer and its answers, in prosperity and success. Most of all, one becomes a Unity minister through an awakening to truth."

Following their ordination, Unity ministers are members of the Unity Ministers' Association, a body representing the 260 Unity centers and dedicated to Christ consciousness in ministerial work and worship. The UMA is quite independent from Unity headquarters, although its secretary is an employee of the Unity School. It elects its own officers and executive board, has its own constitution, sponsors regional meetings, general conferences, and special projects. One of its chief aims is to effect mutually productive relationship between the centers and Unity Village.

One way of implementing this relationship is for the centers to send students and teachers to the Unity Training School conducted during prescribed periods for the development of a workable knowledge of "truth applicable to everyday life." Terms run for four weeks, offer both required and elective courses, and graduation requires a minimum of sixteen credits secured through the equivalent of four years' attendance.

Since a school term was in progress during my Unity stay, I thought I would drop around on this Monday morning to audit one of the classes. As I was about to enter the chapel room in the Silent Unity building where the class was meeting, I paused with my hand on the door, for it was eleven o'clock and the sound of a gong had sounded over a loudspeaker. This was the signal for prayer, the moment when all activity is momentarily suspended and when every employee and visitor stands in reverent silence. On every working day at this hour, the recorded voice of Charles Fillmore recites the Lord's Prayer.

As a visitor to Unity Village, you learn instinctively that wherever you are at eleven o'clock, you enter into the spirit of this two-minute period. Whatever you are doing, you put your work aside, close your eyes, and remain in thought until the prayer is ended.

Not until you catch the spirit of Unity will you understand

how Unity works. And the eleven o'clock prayer time helps you to catch that spirit.

Entering the chapel room at the close of the prayer, I found some forty men and women from various centers, including a woman from Trinidad and a young couple from Latin America. They were here preparing themselves for better service in their respective centers and looking forward to becoming accredited teachers. Sometimes the centers finance their training period, but it is not uncommon for each delegate to take care of his own expenses as he enrolls for these courses in Truth, courses which include "Fundamentals of Unity Principles," "Christian Healing," "Lessons in Truth," "Bible Interpretation," "Lectures on Prayer," "Public Speaking," "Music," and many more.

The tone of these classes is more like that of a spiritual retreat than a college course. Some teachers at Unity are obviously more popular than others and certain Unity ministers in the field return by special request to teach at training sessions and at ministerial conferences, but unlike secular schools, there is a good deal of anonymity in the Unity educational structure. Personalities are never built up nor do we find the academic emphasis which would be fundamentally a part of traditional seminary programs.

Unity is by no means a personality cult. Even Charles and Myrtle Fillmore, respected and honored as they are, have never been "canonized." Papa Charley's eleven o'clock prayer is about all that has ever evolved in this respect. Few unbreakable precedents have been established here at Unity Village or out in the field, and no ironclad creeds have been forged throughout Unity's growing years. Its most popular affirmations have been kept authorless. You will never find a writer's name in the daily meditations in *Daily Word*. It seemed to me as I sat among the students on this Monday morning, that such things as jealousy and an urge for recognition, though these are bound to exist wherever personalities are involved, are kept at a minimum at Unity.

Teachers usually join the staff because they are drawn by the Unity spirit. That is to say, the atmosphere and operational methods are more attractive than are salary or prestige. Also there is opportunity for creative expression and academic freedom quite unmatched on theological campuses.

An excellent example of this is found in the Wee Wisdom school where the Montessori method of teaching has been introduced to children of the Lee's Summit and Kansas City area. Capably conducted by Mrs. Elizabeth Caspari and her Ceylonese associate, Miss Lena Vickramaratne, the school is housed in the former home of Charles and Myrtle Fillmore. Although not actually affiliated with Unity, the Wee Wisdom school is making a strong bid to introduce a form of spiritual and intellectual training which may one day prove to be Unity's contribution to the American educational system in a very real way. It is in the Unity tradition and in the full spirit of freedom in the search for learning and truth.

Retreats, too, are part of the educational training service and these are usually week-long programs built around spiritual inspiration and fellowship. One of the most inspiring retreats is the summer conference of the Youth of Unity, attended by teen-agers from centers in the United States and Canada. Most of these delegates have been trained in the marvelous Sunday Schools which are part of Unity's work. While they gather for serious study at Unity Village, they have ample time to make the most of the recreational facilities: swimming, golfing, and hikes within the enchanting Unity grounds.

There is a veritable year-round schedule of retreats: Lenten retreats, Vacation retreats, Men of Unity retreats, Fall, Thanksgiving, Christmas, and special retreats.

"A retreat," says Unity, "may be a vacation to some, a time for study to others, an opportunity for joining old friends or making new friends of like mind. It may be a way of gaining freedom from the pressures of the world, but it is most of all a time for fulfillment of your particular spiritual need."

Through the years a great bond has sprung up between the Youth of Unity and the workers at Unity Village, a bond which strengthens the lines of communication between the centers and the headquarters. Retreatants are continually impressed with the fact that most of the people in key teaching or managerial positions have been with Unity for an average of twenty-five years and that they originally offered their services without any thought of financial reward.

I realized this anew when, during my Monday interviews, I discussed Unity's golden years with Retta M. Chilcott who, as office manager and personnel director of Unity School, has had an important part in them. What are Unity's "golden years"? All of them!

I felt the loyalty of service to the movement when I talked to author James Dillet Freeman, Unity's best known biographer, poet, and historian. I caught its spirit whenever I met Unity's unusually capable superintendent of printing operations, Alex Alberg, who lives and loves the Unity way of life. I was reminded of it when I talked with members of the teaching and editorial staffs. I sensed it when I visited with Roderick Friend, head of publicity, and when I saw the films and art work which chronicle the march of Unity since the movement began.

I caught something of the application of Unity's philosophy when I visited with music master Carl Frangkiser. Forty years ago this highly skilled musician, disillusioned with religion and disquieted by the way of the world, turned his back on any attempt to figure things out "religiously." However, after a period of military service in World War I, he came out of the army with a questing spirit. When he heard Charles Fillmore, he was persuaded that this approach to faith was what he needed and wanted, and so he offered his services to the Unity cause.

Carl is known to every summer visitor as the conductor of the 60-piece band which plays its concerts in the Unity amphitheatre every summer Sunday night. But most of all, he is responsible for many Unity hymns and for the melody which is the theme song for TV's *Daily Word*. He is composer of many hymn tunes adapted to lyrics written by Unity ministers. One of these, an offering song, with words by Francis J. Gable, gave me a good idea of the Unity point of view:

> I give my offering to God, because He gives to me,
> I praise and bless it with His love, from lack I set it free;
> I trust in God for all my good, He is my rich supply,
> My gift is blessed with love divine, that it may multiply;
> I give the labor of my hand, the thoughts of mind and heart;
> And so in all the Father's work I have a happy part.

It seemed to me that the hymns of Unity were an indispensable part of the educational training program, for their words tell the story of what Unity believes. Take a melody such as *Sun of My Soul* and you will find the words to be Unity's familiar *Prayer of Faith*:

> God is my help in every need,
> God does my every hunger feed,
> God walks beside me, guides my way
> Through every moment of the day.

> I now am wise, I now am true,
> Patient, kind, and loving, too;
> All things I am, can do, and be,
> Through Christ the Truth that is in me;

> God is my health, I can't be sick;
> God is my strength, unfailing, quick;
> God is my all, I know no fear,
> Since God and Love and Truth are here.
>
> HANNAH MORE KOHAUS

The Doxology, known to every Christian as *Praise God from Whom All Blessings Flow,* takes on a new note in Unity when it says:

> Praise God that Good is everywhere,
> Praise to the Love we all may share;
> The Life that thrills in you and me:
> Praise to the Truth that sets us free.

Though this may seem a far cry from the hymnody of the historic faiths, it is an indication of how Unity seeks to bring religion into the idiom of our time.

It does this also by popularizing the *Daily Word* in the five minute TV presentation featured by Rosemary Grace. Anyway you look at it, this program is a Unity vignette and is a mighty force in the training program. It has practical hints for good living, carries with it the luster and charm of faith, and is as non-commercial as a program can be.

Radio, too, is part of Unity's program and this is certainly to be expected since Charles Fillmore established the first radio station in Kansas City. Always alert to ways and means of catching people's imagination, Papa Charley arranged his most popular program from two to four A.M. "When other stations are off the air, that is when I want to be on," was his policy and he had a coast-to-coast audience that joined him regularly in the stillness of the night.

Today Unity radio programs are heard on more than 65 stations with an estimated listening audience of more than three million in the United States, Canada, Panama, and Puerto Rico. The most popular program is called Unity Viewpoint. Scripts prepared at Unity headquarters are made available to center leaders who, in turn, present the material over local stations. Great freedom is allowed in their use. Ministers may make whatever changes they wish, may promote it as best they can, and may or may not give Unity headquarters credit for its preparation.

That is how Unity works through what I have called the Department of Educational Training, third in the structure of this religious movement.

It works also through the Farm which is the fourth factor in the Unity conformation. The Farm is really the Village and the Village is the Farm, and some day the orchards may have to give way to buildings as once the rough rural acreage gave way to the orchards when Unity first came. The Farm is the land, God's land, and it is ready and waiting for whatever use it may be put to in the evolution of the Unity way.

The Farm supplies fruit and vegetables for the Unity household, and there is a fruit stand on the highway where apples, cider, honey, and vegetables may be purchased. But the farm as a farm is financially unproductive. It is what it is holding in escrow for Unity's future that makes it important.

More than fifty years ago, Charles Fillmore predicted that Jackson County, Missouri, would some day be a great spiritual center. He was quite right. Some thirty-five years ago he set a field stone in a vacant lot at 47th and Jefferson, which is now Country Club Plaza, and predicted that one day a mighty temple would rise for the Unity Society. He was also right about that, for today Kansas City's Unity Temple, with its 102' tower and its 68 stained glass windows, and containing 57,000 square feet of floor space, stands on this very spot. A million dollar center, it was dedicated debt free in 1960.

But Charles Fillmore was most prophetic when, in 1920, he looked over the rugged, rolling beauty of the woodland acres and said, "This is what we have been seeking."

Many a visitor will say the same thing. I said it on my Monday at Unity as I walked far out across the grounds into country where I felt a thousand miles from the world. I said it when I walked beside the lake and later sat alone in the amphitheatre where the poplars are companionable, and the mood is strangely holy. The long, winding roads, the greenhouse standing against the restful sight of woodland unimpaired, the inspiring sight of the Tower always seen by day or night, seemed to be saying, "Be still and know!" this, no doubt, is what we have been seeking.

Incidentally, when you add the height of the Tower, 165 feet, to the altitude of the terrain, you get 1200 feet. This altitude, according to many mystics is considered most ideal for meditation, inspiration, and spiritual development. I do not know whether the founders of the movement knew this fact or not. I rather think they would simply have said that if this is true, God had it planned that way.

For that is how Unity works.

CHAPTER FIVE

Unity's Place in the World of Faiths

During my Unity visit, I relived a scene in which I first shared more than twenty years ago. I stood on the top of the Tower with W. Rickert Fillmore as I had done when Unity Village was young, when, in fact, it was still called Unity Farm.

In those days there were only two buildings standing amid great expanses of wooded land in a countryside that seemed hardly ready to be awakened from its rural sleep. Now one could see the cities coming—Kansas City, Lee's Summit, Raytown—with highways and industries and homes and the insistent sound and sight of buildings, buildings everywhere, with only peaceful Unity Village holding off the whirling world. Unity's lake, Unity's amphitheatre, Unity's golf course, Unity's orchards, Unity's meadows; these kept out the thunder of change and made me feel that I was standing in the shelter of tranquility while the hurricane of growth gathered ever more speed. Of course, Unity, too, had grown, but it had evolved, not exploded.

Remembrance wove a subtle magic. In a way it seemed like a thousand years, almost like another lifetime in which I had looked from this vantage point across an architect's unfolding dream. Or it might have been just yesterday, so vivid was my recollection of this man, W. Rickert Fillmore and his mission.

Second son of the founders, Charles and Myrtle Fillmore, "Rick" had become one of my special friends. I had no idea back in those early days of my research that our paths would cross so often. Little did I think that Rick would even recall the time he had left his crews of workmen to climb the Tower with me, an uninvited religious sleuth in search of clues about a new religion.

Rick was the dreamer and the engineer behind the construction of what he seemed to think of as a modern city of God. I remembered his words when, years ago, he gestured with his hat to the scene below, "Everything here, everything you see, is but the physical counterpart of the spiritual process of Unity teaching."

He impressed me as being not only the builder of a village, but the architect of a firm, decisive faith, fit for our time. A story came to mind, a favorite of mine, told descriptively by Zechariah. "I lifted up mine eyes . . . and behold a man with a measuring line in his hand. And I said, Whither goest thou? And he said, To measure Jerusalem, to see what is the breadth thereof, and what is the length thereof. And, behold, an angel went out to meet him, and said to him, Run, speak to this young man saying, Jerusalem shall be inhabited as a town without walls . . . for I, saith the Lord, will be unto her a wall of fire round about, and will be the glory in the midst of her!"

That is how Rick must have seen the phenomenal world, as the mirror of the real. It was God's world, a world without walls, without fear, without division, and without strife. Had anyone asked him, "How can all this be? What do you do for protection against the enemies of sin, sickness, and the evil bent of men?" There would have been but one answer, "Jerusalem shall be inhabited as a town without walls . . . for I, saith the Lord, will be the glory in the midst of her."

Such was the conviction with which Rick had always impressed me. The blueprints from which he worked were mental images of the things he saw and felt within his vision of the city of God.

Once more I stood with him. He was still the tall, compelling, outward-going, deep-thinking man who lived determinedly in two worlds at once, the world of structured things and the world of imagination. Fully at home in each, he evidently had unseen helpers who were as real to him as mortal friends, and no doubt he saw cosmic paths as clearly as he saw the lanes which wound through Unity Village.

Rick was the composer of what I referred to as the harmony and the instrumentation of the Unity surroundings. The score he created had the same kind of rugged gentleness you found in him. It also had the dominant tones that tempered his thinking about life. His brother Lowell had the mysticism of the East with its passive, reflective ebb and flow; Rick had the experientialism of the West with its activism and its knack for getting things done.

Rick left the carefully disciplined life with its early rising, its regular hours, its vegetarianism and the like to Lowell. He was not averse to eating a good steak or sleeping late as his father had done—because he worked half the night—or being active in service clubs and art clubs and social affairs. Lowell might let his ideals carry him away; Rick took a deliberate, scientific view of things. Lowell was the poet; Rick was the builder, but both were their father's sons and through each the will of their parents was kept at work in Unity.

I realized this again when, in commenting on my appraisal of Unity Village, Rick remarked, "Father once said it was all to be the fulfillment of prophecy."

Twenty odd years ago he had told me the very same words. But now he added, "The fact of the matter is, Unity fills a need, and father saw that need long before many others saw it."

"The need for what?"

"For all that Unity teaches. For seeing the good in all religions, for one thing. You are not going to get people to be exclusive about religion when science and culture and everything else are reminding us of the unity of the whole cosmic plan. There is good in all religions and Unity recognizes that good."

He was right, but I wondered whether even Rick with his intuitive insight or Charles Fillmore with all his precognition had foreseen the role Unity might actually play in the world of faiths. Did Lowell realize it, I wondered? Were Unity ministers in the field or the workers in the various departments aware of the challenge that confronted Unity in these modern times?

Did they know that during the past ten years the unity of religions had advanced more rapidly than it had in the past ten hundred? Had they followed the progress of the ecumenical movement and did it matter to them that for the first time since the days of the Reformation, Protestants and Catholics were beginning to discuss their differences?

Even though all this was in the spirit of Unity, I had often felt that Unity as a religious movement stood apart from these events, as complacent as Unity Village itself stands in the center of the teeming world.

As we stood there, I remembered that Unity had no intention of proselytizing or of bringing all religions together under one roof. I reminded myself that it was "unity in diversity" that Unity stressed, but I imagined, too, that I saw a prophetic scene from Unity Tower: the meeting of the World Council of Churches in New Delhi, India, in 1961, when Russian, Polish, Rumanian and Bulgarian Orthodox groups were welcomed to the Council in an unprecedented advent of understanding. I had never heard leaders in the

Unity movement even talk about this ecumenical achievement, but now I wanted to tell them what I saw from the Tower and urge them to recognize the fact that Unity had come into the world for such a time as this.

I saw the bearded Russian Archbishop Nicodim stride to the rostrum as he did at New Delhi, as if the huge golden cross dangling at his breast had power to set ajar the formidable gates of the Iron Curtain. I heard the great crowd of spectators applaud. I saw Christians shake hands and embrace each other while cameras flashed and reporters sent their messages around the globe proclaiming that a mighty step toward *unity* had been achieved. I beheld the Roman Catholic prelates as they stood in the New Delhi crowd watching as if they sensed that the polemics which had despoiled the house of Christendom since 1054 might at long last be somewhat resolved.

In my telescopic view of the religious world, I also saw Pope John XXIII issuing his own ecumenical call. Loud and clear, he called for unity. Anglicanism listened. Anglo-Catholicism was stirred by the invitation. Other factions of the divided and querulous family of faith were beginning to speak to one another for the first time since the days of Henry the Eighth.

Unity was in the air, but did Unity know it? Had the man Charles Fillmore, a modern mystic, an extraordinary ordinary man with a strange prophetic grasp on things, foreseen it? Is that how he inspired his son Rick to take a measuring line in his hands and plot a city of God to see about the length and breadth thereof? "Listen, engineer, what about a wall?" And the angel said, "Run, speak to this young man, saying, Jerusalem shall be inhabited as a town without walls . . . for I, saith the Lord, will be unto her a wall of fire round about, and will be the glory in the midst of her!"

It may be that Unity saw the job ahead. It could have

been that this was why Rick said, "You are not going to get people to be exclusive about religion any longer." Vision or real, perhaps Unity did recognize the fact that the whole vast world with its teeming billions and its milieu of social concerns was moving toward understanding. Ecumenicity was in the air, not only among religious leaders but more particularly among the masses, and it was for the masses that the Unity movement was geared.

If Rick had the vision, then Rick's son, Charles Rickert Fillmore, has it, too, and he is in a position to do something about it. A member of the Board of Directors of Unity School and manager of the Public Relations department, Charlie, as he is affectionately called, has the full dimension of Unity's future at heart. His home is "The Arches," the dwelling romantically associated with the life of Myrtle Fillmore. Here Charlie, with his wife Anne, and their two children, is deeply conscious of his responsibility in the continuity of the Fillmore tradition.

Charlie's work and concern for the movement have taken him on several swings around the American Unity circuit for the purpose of getting firsthand information on how the headquarters can most effectively serve the 260 established centers and how, in turn, the centers can best assist the headquarters in the general areas of learning, research, and development in a day when the Unity School is challenged by a trend toward unity throughout the Christian world.

As Rick's son scans the American scene, so Rick's daughter, Rosemary, is dedicating herself more and more to a world view of Unity. Married to a prominent Lee's Summit realtor, Stanley Grace, Rosemary, as the "Voice of Unity," is featured on 70 TV stations. Her daily, five-minute program consisting of the reading of *Daily Word*, together with a commentary, had been a studio type program for many years, but in 1962 Rosemary launched forth on a globe-circling tour familiarizing herself with other cultures and keynoting the spiritual oneness of the people of the world. In a very real way, this attractive mother of two children is Unity's first world-wide "missionary" in a modern role. Political leaders like Nasser and Nehru, and countries from the Union of Soviet Socialist Republics to the Free Territory of Hong Kong have now heard about the Unity movement, many for the first time.

Rosemary learned from her global tour, as her brother Charles Rickert learned from his American travels, that the impulse toward genuine understanding is basic in every culture and that the unity among men and the unity of the spirit are beginning to appear as converging lines.

From my conversations with both Charlie and Rosemary, I gathered that they know that the Unity movement will have to evolve against the background of an evolving ecumenical Christendom. This was not true in the days of Charles and Myrtle Fillmore, but it is true now, and there is no doubt that Unity has contributed mightily to the trend. However, the challenge confronting the Unity movement is greater now than it was in the days of Papa Charley. That it will be equally great in the days ahead is easily foreseen. For when the wounds between Roman Catholic and Eastern Catholic have been healed, there will still remain the wounds between Catholics and Protestants, and between Protestants and Protestants, and between Christians and non-Christians, and most of all there will still be the wounds between man and man.

Unity does not believe in wounds. It prefers to see the love and hope that exist between all these groups, and I saw this vision, too, as I stood on Unity Tower. I was looking not into a Village, but into a world, a magnificent, mysterious world, the venturesome world of the quest for truth, a world which had never been fully explained or thoroughly comprehended.

There was something purposeful behind this world, though we could not always fathom the purpose. There was something of infinite planning behind it, though we might still be hazy about the ultimate plan. There was divine meaning behind it, though to some of us the meaning remained unclear no matter how many prophets heaven had sent. Like the search for truth, the search for meaning in the world was a quest, and men had always, at all times, been looking for the city of God, and occasionally one, more daring than the rest, had gone out with a measuring line in his hand and had heard the angel's voice.

"Rick," I said, "do you know what I see from this Tower?"

"Well," he answered, "I see new things every time I come up here."

"Men," I told him.

"What kind of men?"

"Men on a quest."

"Well, of course," he agreed, "that's the whole idea."

"I used to say that truth is where you find it, but recently I met a Unity student who said, 'Truth is where you seek it.' That comes even closer to my point of view. Religion's answers are found in the seeking."

"Well," Rick mused, "there is nothing wrong with that, is there?"

No, there was nothing wrong with that, but I wanted to make sure that Unity realized that it was a hub in the ecumenical wheel, not an ecumenicity of polity and creed, but an ecumenicity of the spirit.

I did see men from the Tower. Plato, for example, who, four hundred years before the Christian era held as his thesis a world of divine types, archetypes or ideas which he defined as the permanent and the real. All else was but an ephemeral and imperfect representation. The idea of the Good was the highest and noblest of all ideals and it was this Platonic conception which Unity had caught. Perfect virtue consisted in a knowledge of the Good, and the deeper the knowledge the greater the goodness.

Anyone could see Plato walking the Unity grounds. A

contemporary follower of this Greek philosopher could feel at home in Unity. He could bring with him his most cherished Platonic ideals and find them harmonized in Unity's teachings. When Plato said, "Since God is Good He is not the Author of *all* things, but He is the cause of the *good* only," he contributed to Charles Fillmore's basis for his theory that the cause of evil must be sought elsewhere than in God's goodness.

I could also see Confucius in the Unity setting and hear him say, "The good man in his dealings with the world has neither enmities or affections. Wherever he sees the right, he seeks to identify himself with the right."

The Buddha, who lived some six hundred years before the time of Christ, suggested an eightfold path which could have led straight into Unity Village. He admonished his followers to observe: Right Views, Right Intentions, Right Speech, Right Action, Right Livelihood, Right Effort, Right Mindfulness, Right Concentration. Though Unity was Christ-centered, there were those who, as good Buddhists, found the consciousness of Gautama Buddha involved in much that Unity sought to teach, the denial of sentimentally placed generosity or misplaced charity, for example. These were Buddhistic, but they were Unity, too.

I could also see Zoroaster in the Unity setting. This Persian seer, older than any other ancient sage, once said of healing, "He who heals with the Holy Word, this man is best." And that, in effect, is what Charles Fillmore said.

He also voiced many things which the master mystic Pythagoras enunciated long years before the time of Christ. When this mighty-minded Greek proclaimed that, "All men know what they want, but few know what they need," he was putting his thoughts into Charles Fillmore's mind, as he was when he announced that, "We must drive sickness from the body, ignorance from the soul, luxury from the senses, discord from the family, and excess from all of life."

Unity was the recipient of the teachings of all faiths. Judaism conferred on it the promises of divine law. Islam shared with it the power of the inspired word. Shinto gave it the tender touch of gentleness. Jainism breathed into it a reverence for all life. Hinduism imparted to it its belief in reincarnation and the karmic law. When Taoism said, "Prize compassion, therefore you will be able to be fearless. Prize frugality, therefore be able to be liberal. Prize modesty, therefore be able to be a leader of men," I could almost hear Charles Fillmore speak the words.

Yet it was, of course, Christianity in which Unity found the heartland of its beliefs. The words of philosophers and seers were important and the utterances of prophets were inter-related in the common cause of truth, but Jesus Christ was the fountain from which the living words and the living truth flowed into Unity.

"Many have caught sight of the fact that the true church of Christ is a state of consciousness in man," said Charles Fillmore, "but few have gone so far in the realization as to know that in the very body of each and every man and woman is a temple in which Christ holds religious services at all times. 'Ye are a temple of God' is not a symbolical appellation, but a statement of architectural truth. Under the direction of the Christ, a new body is constructed by the thinking faculty in man; the material entering into this superior structure are the spiritualized organic substances, and the new creation is the temple or body of spirit." Unity proclaimed itself as a metaphysical school that taught the use of the Jesus Christ doctrine in everyday life and opened each class session with the words, "Jesus Christ is the head of Unity School. We are now open, receptive, and obedient to His instruction and guidance."

With this receptivity it could not help but synthesize the expression of many Christian groups in its formation. The fervor of early Methodism ran through its history. The mysticism of Catholicism played its part in its metaphysical plan. Elements of Christian Science and Divine Science were apparent in its concept of Truth. The great religions, old as those fashioned after Zoroaster and new as those inspired by Baha'u'llah, found points of similarity and contact in Unity. The mind power of the ancients, the will power of the prophets, the God power of the medieval fathers of the faith, the positive thinking of the most modern purveyors of holy writ, all wove the fabric of their belief into the Unity pattern.

As I stood on the Tower with Rick Fillmore and thought of all this, a prayer came to mind, a prayer increasingly used by liberal churches and descriptive of Unity's place in the great religions of the world:

> "Almighty God, help us with heart and mind to build the church universal, where there is place for all ancient wisdom and all modern thought; which finds in all prophecies a harmony, in all scriptures a unity, and in all life a reflection of Thy will.
>
> Which rejects all that separates and divides and respects all that leads to brotherhood and peace.
>
> Which believes in freedom in the search for truth, love in the administration of justice, and individual discipline in the social order.
>
> Which shall make of all sects, classes, nations and races one fellowship and in which the spirit of man shall be recognized as Thy Spirit. Toward this ideal, O God, give us the vision and the courage to earnestly strive."

Rick saw this church, as I saw it, from the Tower. He saw it as he walked among men, as he read scientific journals, and as he developed his creative ideas. I felt that every forward-looking Unity student saw it, a church universal which already existed in consciousness.

It included the physicist whose thoughts have penetrated outer space, the historian whose study has followed the footprints of God through the rise and fall of civilizations, the scientist who has unlocked the secret doors of the inner mind, the philosopher who has spied a harmony in the once inharmonious schools of thought, the educator who perceives a divine power beyond, no less than within the intellectual process, the industrialist who has caught on to a workable ethic in his business dealings, the theologian who recognizes a divine power as the common ground of all being; in short, it embraces men and women of every walk of life who have begun to realize that religion is a quest, an adventure in search and discovery—all these constitute a dispersed spiritual potential, the new church, which has yet to be made collective.

For Unity knew, as I knew, that above and beyond the things that separate various religions are truths which unite them, and that while many groups are divided by nonessentials, the great essentials are being discovered, often outside the bounds of the institutionalized, traditional denominations.

"I lifted up mine eyes . . . and behold a man with a measuring line in his hand. And behold an angel went out to meet him, and said to him . . . Jerusalem shall be inhabited as a town without walls . . . for I, saith the Lord, will be the glory in the midst of her!"

It occurred to me that if I were to ask any sincere, thinking person what he is looking for in the way of a vital, contemporary religion, he would tell me something like this: I think religion should keep a person healthy in body, active in mind, and joyful in spirit. It should assist him in maintaining that fine balance between loving the world and denying the world, of enjoying the world without losing the spiritual perspective, of being successful in the world without making success a final goal, and of prospering in the world while remaining consciously poor and humble of spirit. Give me a faith that makes demands of me and one of which I can make demands. Give me a faith that has the Christ in it. Not a vague, theological, dogmatic Christ, but One who lives and walks with men. Give me techniques and affirmations, and words to live by, and, most of all, give me examples of the workability of faith in living people so that I may better see what I, too, may become.

Unity, as an eclectic faith, could fill this prescription. Like America, it was an amalgam and therein lay its genius and its strength. As America had absorbed the cultures of the world and had benefited by the very best motives of the world's people, Unity had profited by the thought and discoveries of the world's religions. I would guess that it had received much because it had given much, and this, of course, was basic as a Unity principle.

The God of Unity was so great that He could never express himself fully in one denomination or compress Himself into one exclusive sect. He was a prism through which the one light was refracted. He was the sea from which and into which the rivers of thought were flowing. He was the love eternal, out of which love in its myriad forms expressed itself. He was God and, being God, He was strictly universal.

I was reminded again that you can be a good member of Unity and still worship in other faiths, for the object of worship is always God as principle, God as love, and God as good. You can sit yoga fashion, if you wish, or enter the satori of Zen and say your prayers, and be a Unity follower. You can walk the eightfold path of the Buddha without straying from Unity teaching and beliefs. You can bow five times toward Mecca, as the Moslems do, and still be Unity conscious. You can stand before the tomb of your ancestors, as do the Confucianist and the Taoist; you can say a prayer of gratitude for the influence and heritage of a departed loved one without denying what Unity believes. You can sit before the sacred fire of the Parsees and gaze into the holy flames, if the Parsi priest will let you, and you can enter into the spirit of Parseeism without losing your Unity point of view. You can stand with the Jew over the holy Torah, or walk with the Shintoist through his sacred groves, or chant an affirmation with the Hindu on the banks of the Ganges— you can do all these things and still be a student of Unity because there is within you a living flame of truth which warms you with the knowledge that the spirit of God is one spirit, and that He is sovereign over all creeds.

As the Christ becomes greater to you in Unity, the Buddha also becomes greater, and the greater the Buddha becomes, the greater the Christ becomes. That is true of your estimate of all prophets when you know the prophet Jesus Christ. He who lives in all, lives in you, and because He lives, all people live more gloriously, more richly, and with more subtle meaning than they lived before. There are those who will not understand this paradox, but most Unity students understand it and live by it as an expression of truth.

"I am grateful to Unity," a man in the Detroit center once said to me, "for giving me a way of life that fears no other ways of life. I am grateful for its approach to all religions, Christian and non-Christian alike. Like food, like music, or like languages, religion is universal, and I am glad that Unity taught me this truth. I don't have to join any other religion to get the benefit of that religion, nor does anyone have to join Unity, for that matter, to get what Unity has to offer."

There was some logic in this, to be sure. During my tramping among the religions of the world, I had found Americans who, in their quest for a meaningful faith, have tried to become Hindus. They transplanted themselves to India and I saw them there, American women wearing Indian saris, and American men wrapped in *dhotis*, walking barefooted in the holy ashrams. Sincere they were, there was no doubt about it, but it occurred to me that to follow Devi or Krishna you need not actually become like them any more than you must look and dress like Jesus in order to follow his principles in modern life. The prophets and avatars should be challenges to our character, not tests for physical imitation.

In southeast Asia I found Americans who aspired to become Buddhist monks. They donned saffron robes, discarded their shoes, shaved their heads and embraced the vows, but they still looked like Americans and thought like Americans and often, I dare say, secretly longed for America. It is difficult, if not painful, for a westerner to sit lotus fashion as the Buddha sat or to assume the postures which the yogis put themselves into. Not that we should not try it and not that yoga is not helpful and therapeutic, but you cannot transplant individuals any more than you can transplant tropical trees to the Arctic. There are exceptions, to be sure, but generally each thrives best in the area to which it is indigenous. Unity bids us be true not only to the color of our skin, but to the color of our culture, especially we Americans, because here we have the color and culture of the world, the blending of all groups, the fusion of all nationalities, the embodiment of all religions.

It was like the city of God which Zechariah saw when he said, "Run, speak to this young man, saying, Jerusalem shall be inhabited as a town without walls, for I, saith the Lord, will be unto her a wall of fire. . . ."

I thought a good deal about this city of God as I stood on the Tower. I also thought a good deal about our nation during this Unity moment, for here the stars and stripes are always flying high on the mast of the Unity Village quadrangle.

There is at least this much to be said about Unity and our country: other religions came to America seeking freedom; Unity came with freedom seeking America. It came with freedom in its search for truth, freedom in its organizational pattern, freedom in its willingness to explore, and in its affirmative pronouncements which bear upon the whole broad doctrine of mankind.

Other religions came seeking to build a church, to convert the "heathen," to point out to their fellow Christians where they might be wrong. Unity came pointing out where they might be right.

Unity came as a healing faith. An auxiliary faith. A truth-seeking faith. A Christ-centered faith with the kind of charity it believed had been demonstrated by the Man of Galilee.

Unity came helping people to be "overcomers." It assisted men to overcome the cause for greed, the cause for suffering, the cause for sin. Unity literature and Unity teaching has little reference to sin, original sin or sins of commission or sins of omission. Its purpose is to point out that men are not in their true nature sinners, but sons of God, created in the image and likeness of God, and it is toward helping men regain this knowledge of their divine perfection that Unity directs its efforts.

That is how it came into being. That is how it grew, and that is how it develops and expands despite the fact that it now has its churches and temples and centers across the wide reaches of the land. I dare say that if any Unity minister had to choose between perpetuating his church and preaching his truth, he would unhesitatingly choose the latter. In fact, he has chosen it, and the church he serves is a non-sectarian fellowship of those who have found the way of Unity.

I found an analogy for all this whenever I thought of my summer place in British Columbia, Canada. It is situated on a promontory overlooking Kootenay Lake. Flowing through this four-mile wide, 100-mile long expanse of blue water is a river, the Kootenay, which gives the lake its name, its color, and its substance. This river, which has never been accurately measured, is part of the lake and the lake is part of it. The river is deep, silent, and uncommonly strong. It nourishes the lake, but, in a way, the lake with its many mountain streams also nourishes the river. It is all quite reciprocal.

If you imagine the lake to be America, particularly America with its spiritual consciousness, then Unity is the river; silent, unmeasurable, strong, nourishing and being nourished as it flows steadily through the shifting moods of our nation's religious life. Who is to guess its influence? Who is to say that this is where Unity ends and this is where Protestantism or Catholicism begins? It is also all quite reciprocal.

Unity has grown because it meets a people's needs. It is a teaching faith that has proved to be, in this scientific age, doctrinally acceptable, but the emphasis has never been a doctrinal one. It has been a practical one. Charles Fillmore believed and practiced what he taught and attracted to his teaching others who believed and practiced. Unity is the story of the river and the lake.

The number of Unity centers has grown and continues to grow, but the number of people who affiliate themselves with these centers as members has not grown in proportion to the number of people who read and study Unity literature. Unity headquarters is unlike most denominational offices in that it is not actually interested in membership. It is irrelevant to Unity whether or not a person "belongs" to the movement. There is as yet no word to identify a Unity student such as there is to designate a Presbyterian or a Methodist or a Lutheran or a Catholic. Terms like "Unitist" or "Unitite" or "Unity-arian" and even "Unitick" (!) have been suggested, but none of these cumbersome names ever became popular. Unity followers still prefer to be known simply as Truth students or Unity students or followers of Unity or, simply, Christians of the Judeo-Christian tradition.

Christians they surely are! Yet a serious study of the literature of Unity will reveal the universal influence of the major religions of the world. And anyone who stands on the Tower, as I did with Rick, will catch the Biblical vision of the Judean prophet when he said, "I lifted up mine eyes . . . and behold a man with a measuring line in his hand . . . And an angel went out to meet him and said . . . Jerusalem shall be inhabited as a town without walls . . . for I, saith the Lord, will be unto her a wall of fire round about, and I will be the glory in the midst of her!"

CHAPTER SIX

The Unity Approach
to Prosperity

On Thursday morning at Unity Village I awoke to the sound of rain on the motel roof. "God's rain," I caught myself saying and was reminded again that in the Unity environment you need never be ashamed of religious sentimentality.

God's rain, for example.

Or other things. Like prayers, shall we say.

Many are the prayers I have prayed at public meetings, at convocations on college campuses, at banquets, at church conventions, but just now it seemed to me that among the most beautiful of all prayers was one I heard Unity children pray one rainy morning, "Our happy hearts just sing and sing! We thank Thee, God, for everything!"

For everything. Even for the sound of rain on the roof. Unity has a subtle way of returning worldlings to an age of religious innocence.

The big, impersonal world loses some of its bite in Unity, the issues of life become less culpable, and a person's goals become more clear. Even prosperity, which is the passionate dream of men, is put into a perspective so unusual that callous skeptics have been tempted to experiment with Unity's approach to it. In Unity you are assured that money can be the root of *good* as well as of evil. You need never think of good business as being outside God's sphere, or of success as being beyond your capabilities and reach of mind.

Papa Charley was emphatically articulate about it. He said, "Charge your mind with statements that express plenty. Deny poverty. Praise what you have, be it ever so little, and insist that it is constantly growing larger." That was a great secret. You must bless what you have before you can expect any more than what you've got!

Charles Fillmore looked upon God's gift of money as he did upon God's gift of rain. It was abundantly free, especially to those who understood the working of the law, more especially to those who had the will to receive it, and most especially to those who had the spirit to bless it.

He had his own whimsical parables about how prosperity worked, and one of these, culled from an actual happening in the Deep South, got to be a special favorite of mine.

"There was a pastor in a small church in Georgia," he reported, "who suggested to his congregation of cotton farmers that they dedicate a tenth part of their land to the Lord and ask Him for protection against the ravages of the boll weevil which had devastated the crops in that vicinity for several years. Seven farmers decided to do this. They set aside a tenth part as the Lord's land, and though they took no measures to protect their crop on these dedicated acres, the boll weevil did not attack the cotton there. Furthermore, the quality of the fiber was better on those acres than on any that adjoined them. The experiment was so successful that practically all the farmers in that community decided to follow the plan in the future."

I liked that story and I could almost hear Papa Charley tell it with the whimsical touch he always had. He spoke in the language of his time and his anecdotes made his listeners feel that God was pleased with the telling. He liked to stay close to nature. He looked and listened for the telltale signs of heaven's presence and found them in many places.

God's rain, for example.

And God's land.

And no more boll weevils.

The parable aptly defined Unity's position in relation to both money and "miracles." The regenerated fields were not a supernatural phenomenon. To Fillmore and to Unity they represented the logical results in the sequence of an immutable law. God protects what is His and blesses what is blessed to Him. This was part of God's law and Papa Charley never lost his simple, childlike faith about the law's workability.

Money is a touchstone in the working of this law. It is often *the* touchstone, for there are people all over the world who, as Charles Fillmore well knew, are Christians only up to their hip-pockets. They give the good Lord practically everything they have: advice, excuse, good intentions, even time and a certain amount of energy, everything excepting the coin of the realm. They shy away from stewardship, which is why they are annoyed by boll weevils.

They overlook the fact that they are dealing, not with a supranormal, anthropomorphic God, but with a law, a law which says that money has a spiritual as well as a material side, and that the spiritual is the "cause side." The spiritual side has to do with stewardship whether you are a cotton farmer or a financier. The "cause side" creates the conditions in which you live in your environmental world.

To dwell upon poverty is to create it.

To dwell upon abundance is to attract it.

Spiritual economics do not deal merely with money; they deal with life, because our attitude about life fashions the "money world" in which we live.

If you give grudgingly, you surround yourself with grudging thoughts.

If you give poorly, you remain poor.

You evolve according to the pattern of your thoughts.

Consciousness makes you what you are, and you can make your consciousness.

Later, as I walked through the rain thinking these thoughts it occurred to me that Unity people are never poor, neither in spirit nor in worldly goods. Etched on their hearts is a major tenet in their canon of beliefs, "Wealth of consciousness will express itself in wealth of manifestation." Just now this seemed to me an infallible decree, falling like God's rain, on the unjust and the just, nourishing and refreshing the subsoil of faith in the human heart. "Wealth of consciousness will express itself in wealth of manifestation."

Long ago in my study of Unity I learned a prosperity prescription that consisted of four simple steps:

1. Recognize that there is no lack and that the law of cause and effect operates interdependently in all of life.

2. Affirm thoughts of abundance in the assurance that these thoughts are irrevocably true and workable for you.

3. Translate the thoughts into action.

4. Give thanks for the demonstration of truth.

I never forgot it. *Recognize—Affirm—Translate—Give thanks.* Who could doubt its practical use? Only he who would not try it. Who would call it simple and naive? Only he who missed its implications. Who could limit its power? Only he who put a limit on God. *Recognize—Affirm—Translate—Give thanks.*

Unity's founders lived by this prescription so religiously and demonstrated it so convincingly that it became the polestar by which the growth of Unity was charted. To understand the working of it, it was necessary to recognize one incontrovertable truth: God's substance is unlimited.

Substance in the Unity sense is not to be confused with materiality. Substance is not some *thing* or some entity or some specific material. Substance is the "God stuff," the divine distillate, out of which all reality is formed. Substance was defined by Charles Fillmore as energy, as spirit light, as the intangible essence back of all matter and force.

He launched many a venture without the immediate finances needed for seeing the venture through. Convinced that a plan was God's will and God's vision and God's work, he cast himself in the role of administrator for Him who had in escrow whatever money or material were needed. He knew the formula. He knew the meaning of substance. He never idealized poverty as did the early Christian saints or the Hindu sannyasin or the Buddhist monks. He never sang the song on which I was nurtured during the formative years of my youth:

> "A tent or a cottage,
> What do I care?
> They're building a palace
> For me—over there."

None of the "over there," "pie-in-the-sky" religion ever crept into the Unity movement, not even through the back door. Eternal substance, like eternal life, was here and now waiting to be materialized. Yet Unity's deepest spiritual consciousness was not, in the days of the founders, nor is it now, a money measurement. Never was God looked upon as a servitor from whom one sought a largesse, nor an alchemist who made men rich because they chanted a magical creed. It was the working of the law, the law which affirmed that if you understand the nature of substance and follow the prescription and give the Lord His tithe, the heavens open.

Prosperity is like falling rain.

Consecrate the acres, dedicate the land, and you get rid of boll weevils.

Seek the kingdom for the kingdom's sake, and your needs will be bounteously fulfilled. How bounteously was impressed upon me again as I saw the rain fall over Unity Village.

In 1886, so the story goes, Charles and Myrtle Fillmore lived unknown and unwell in a gabled house on Wabash Avenue in Kansas City. I mention this because I once served a church on 36th and Wabash as student pastor. The Fillmore house was never pointed out to me because Unity had, long ago, outgrown both the house and the district. But I remember how my congregation struggled in those days to make ends meet and how I was often tempted to apply Unity's prosperity technique.

Prosperity affirmations, however, were not yet in my idiom in those days. My consciousness lacked the courage to claim my "heritage." I was not quite ready to say, "Jesus Christ is now here, raising me to His consciousness of the omnipresent, all-providing God substance, and my prosperity is assured!"

When I think of my little vine-covered church on Wabash Avenue (taken over recently by a Negro congregation) and when I remember the huge churches on Linwood Boulevard, the history of Unity becomes ever more graphic and the saga of Charles and Myrtle Fillmore grows increasingly more amazing. They had, as we have said, no intention or desire to compete in the field of Christian faith; they wanted only to complement what the churches taught and to demonstrate the basic tenets which most denominations professed. Yet, any new interpretation or demonstration of religion was, in those days, open to challenge and suspicion. Church Street, U.S.A., especially in its yesterdays, was openly competitive and as far as the institutionalized churches were concerned, money was both a symbol of success and a cause for concern.

Just how *did* the Lord regard prosperity? Some ministers said He condemned it, others said He sanctified it, but no matter what view a minister took he wanted to see his church and his ministry prosper, and financial growth was always a tacit endorsement of the Lord's favor. All of which accounted for the fact that Kansas City churches, no less than congregations elsewhere in America, turned inquisitively to Unity to discover what was making it prosper and grow. Few caught on to the secret and even fewer were willing to understand or to try the prosperity prescription: *Recognize—Affirm—Translate—Give thanks.*

Nonetheless, Charles and Myrtle Fillmore went on demonstrating prosperity according to the four points. The more they gave, the more they got. The more they shared, the more the movement grew.

One of the early co-workers confided to me that many were the times that Papa Charley came to her and said, "There is someone here who needs help, see that he gets work and be sure to give him something to eat." If she insisted there were no jobs and there was nothing to eat, he simply waved his hands and said, "There must be something. There always is."

And there always was.

Where did the job come from? How was the food supplied? God supplied them out of His unmeasurable substance. *Recognize—Affirm—Translate—Give thanks.*

One day Fillmore came to this co-worker and said, "There is a woman here who needs help. Give her a job."

"But we have no jobs to give," was the response.

"Create a job for her," said Fillmore. "She needs money in order to get her dental plates. She is toothless. Give her a job."

What could a toothless woman do? Lick stamps? Papa Charley always had a sense of humor!

He had the light touch.

As light as God's rain.

As honest as sunlight.

As simple as a parable about boll weevils.

Papa Charley's mother figured as strongly in the growth

of Unity as pioneer mothers figured in the conquering of new frontiers. For years she managed the household while Charles and Myrtle carried on their ministry. Truth is, they would have had a difficult time carrying it on without Mother Fillmore's help.

Many were the days that she was elbow deep in soapsuds washing clothes or scrubbing pots and pans, when Charles and Myrtle would come in followed by half-a-dozen bedraggled transients who had professed interest in metaphysical teachings.

"Besides this, they're hungry," Papa Charley would say, and Myrtle would add, "They have a real yearning for the work."

Mother Fillmore suspected they had more of a yearning for a hand-out and a place to sleep.

Often at supper time she would say to Rick or to Lowell, "Look down the street and see how many they are bringing tonight."

She was the true Martha, this hardy mother, and Myrtle was the Mary. Myrtle had so little interest in housework that when son Rick built a home for her in Unity Village, the famous house called *The Arches*, he built it without a kitchen at her request. She wanted a retreat, a place to study and to write, and eating was secondary. But in a house nearby, Mother Fillmore, with indomitable energy and homespun faith in all that Unity taught and believed, saw to it that her daughter-in-law kept body and soul together and that son Charles found ready answers to his prayers through whatever toil and talent she possessed.

Recognize—Affirm—Translate—Give thanks.

That is how Unity grew. It grew as if the Master were seeking to make graphic something He once said about the need for childlike faith.

So they came to Unity, transients who wanted free meals and a bed, businessmen who had tried to beat the game

with their superior cunning and had learned it would not
work, students who wanted a knowledge of truth, women
with time on their hands, scholars who sensed that the
semblance of simplicity in Unity was, in fact, a metaphysical
formula founded on knowledge out of man's enlightened
past. They came, and they were taught and fed and prayed
for and entertained, whether it was a toothless woman or an
Edwin Markham, who stayed for an entire summer. They
came because the magnet of prosperity drew them and
tantalized them and blessed them, while they, in turn,
blessed Unity.

When the work prospered to the point where it gained
world-wide attention, Charles Fillmore had his explanation,
"The Father gives abundantly," he said, "I receive thankfully, and give again generously."

There were "Prosperity Banks" in those days—originated
by the Fillmores in 1910—consisting of a small cardboard
container with a handy slot for contributions. They proved
to be more than a mere depository for small change; their
proper use served as a discipline in the art of giving—and
receiving—with such success that they are still widely used
by Unity followers today.

Anyone may receive a Prosperity Bank for the asking, and
I well remember the first one I got shortly after I left my
church on 36th and Wabash. Truth to say, I was still skeptical
both about the method and the device, but the fullness of
time was dawning. I was drawn to Unity more and more,
and a cardboard "prayer bank" no longer seemed ridiculous
to me. The instructions called for placing a small deposit
in the box each day. At the end of a ten week period or
sooner, the money was to be sent to Unity as a donation,
as a payment for a subscription to a Unity publication, or as
a means of purchasing Unity literature.

Attractively decorated with a picture of Unity Tower, the
bank was embellished with affirmations and appropriate

texts, "Thou, O God, art my mighty resource." "The Spirit of the Lord goes before me, and my Prosperity, Success, and Happiness are assured." There was also a border of stars, one star to be encircled each time a deposit was made.

It seemed a novel idea, and I took it seriously. As close to a prescribed morning hour as practicable, I made it a point to drop a quarter into the bank, meanwhile repeating the required affirmation, "God is in charge of all my affairs, and abundant good is manifested daily for me."

These were depression days and I looked upon money with utmost respect. I truly expected and believed that God *would* manifest abundant good for me by virtue of the fact that an institutionalized Christian such as I had condescended to enter into this unorthodox pact with Him. A quarter a day for the Lord!

I kept my promise as faithfully as if I had seen a copy of the Dedication and Covenant which Charles and Myrtle Fillmore signed when they began their work of faith in 1892. This document, which now hangs on many a Unity wall, would inspire anyone.

We, Charles Fillmore and Myrtle Fillmore, husband and wife, hereby dedicate ourselves, our time, our money, all we have and all we expect to have, to the Spirit of Truth, and through it, to the Society of Silent Unity.

It being understood and agreed that the said Spirit of Truth shall render unto us an equivalent for this dedication in peace of mind, health of body, wisdom, understanding, love, life, and an abundant supply of all things necessary to meet every want without our making any of these things the object of our existence.

In the presence of the Conscious Mind of Christ Jesus, this 7th day of December, A.D. 1892.

Signed,

CHARLES FILLMORE
MYRTLE FILLMORE

That was how Unity began and that is how Unity prosperity was put to work. Certainly, the least I could do was to experiment in my own cautious way with my Prosperity Bank.

I remember how, on a trip to my parental home in Sauk City, Wisconsin, I took the bank with me. There I discovered that our local church had just introduced the envelope system as its money-raising method. My mother, the only woman member on the church consistory, was actively engaged in this latest approach to church finances and she explained that now our members needed only to tuck their weekly contribution into the handy multi-colored envelope and drop it into the collection plate each Sunday morning. She thought it would inspire people to come to the services more regularly. It did. But it also caused some to stay away.

My mother was chairman of the every-member-canvass which put the envelope system into operation, and one Sabbath afternoon her crews fanned out over town, dedicated to the task of persuading church members to pledge a weekly contribution. When I signed my pledge, I shared with my mother the plan of Unity's Prosperity Bank.

"But you don't belong to Unity, I hope!" she said.

I put her mind at rest.

"How much do you put into it?" she asked, with some concern.

"A quarter a day."

"That," she figured, "would be over ninety dollars a year. That is more than some of our richest members give to our church. Why is it that our people don't give the way they should?"

"It's a matter of consciousness," I said.

"Consciousness?" she echoed. "Our people are just too stingy, that's all!"

She examined the Prosperity Bank. It was a new departure for her to think that giving involved a law, and she also felt there was a bit of audacity involved in the declaration, "Divine love bountifully supplies and increases this my offering!" or "I am always provided for because I have faith in God as my omnipresent abundance!" Only someone as orthodox as my mother knew how revolutionary all this sounded to orthodox ears.

One feature about the box impressed her. The ritual. Unity might not have called it a ritual, but my mother did. A ritual. She liked the idea of holding a quarter in her hand, placing the coin part way into the slot, closing her eyes, and whispering a prayer. She loved to pray, especially in German, a language which she was sure was considerably dearer to the Lord than English.

She thought that Unity was wise in combining the giving of the gift with the praying of a prayer. With all her solid religiosity, she had never thought about blessing the contributions she made to the Lord's work. She had her policies, such as never using a gloved hand to drop an offering into the collection plate, never putting in loose change, and certainly never glancing to see what the person seated next to her contributed, unless perhaps it might have been my father. She often quietly checked up on him, but usually she simply closed her eyes and let the offering fall.

Now, as I persuaded her to get the feel of the Prosperity Bank, I asked her to repeat the affirmation, "God is in charge of all my affairs, and abundant good is manifested daily for me." She was a good sport, for I suspect that this was the most positive affirmation my mother had ever said aloud. Fifty years of German evangelical indoctrination had persuaded her that God might *not* be in charge of all her affairs. After all, the devil might have a hand in them. And as for abundant good being manifested daily, she was not so sure about that either. She often felt beset by abundant evil! Furthermore an affirmation of this kind was like putting words into God's mouth or at least telling Him what He ought to do, and our family had been rigorously brought up on "not my will but Thine." But she went through with it. She spoke the words and dropped the coin, and it seemed to me she did it with a sense of real exhilaration.

We often talked about it later as the years of my research developed and as I frequently returned home with reports of what was happening among the new religions which, like Unity, were determinedly elbowing their way into the religious culture of our time.

"There *is* something wrong with us," she would murmur. "There is surely something wrong with our benevolences. Even the envelope system hasn't solved the problem. Our people just simply aren't good givers."

Rummage sales, baked goods sales, soup suppers, pancake suppers, even church bazaars never got the budget over the hump. There was also the period when fast-talking salesmen used the church parlors to demonstrate stainless steel pots and pans, giving the church a seemingly generous cut, but this, too, never seemed to get the blessing of the Lord. Nor the blessing of my mother. She was dead set against turning the church into a "sales barn" as she called it. (Wasn't this why Jesus drove the money changers out of the temple?) When other members of the church consistory said she was old-fashioned, she consoled herself by saying, "Well, I thank God we at least don't have bingo games the way the Catholics do!"

Meantime, Unity was growing. Unity was prospering. *Recognize—Affirm—Translate—Give thanks.* From an office in the Journal Building, to offices in the Deardorf Building, to a suite of offices in the Hall Building, to a functional house on McGee Street, to the new building on Tracy Avenue, complete with a famous inn, administration building, and radio broadcasting facilities, Unity was growing.

God's rain kept coming down.

The boll weevil respected the dedicated acres.

The light touch of love was transforming lives.

Often as I tramped through the American religious scene in my own growing work in those days, I pictured Unity followers playing their innocent and rather lovely game with the Lord, playing it, so far as prosperity was concerned, with dimes and dollars. I visualized them holding prosperity thoughts and I held the thoughts with them, confident that a power was being generated by our corporate act, feeling a warm sense of kinship with people of other lands and other creeds, united in the confidence that "God is in charge of all my affairs, and abundant good is manifested for me daily."

Unity headquarters was a focal point, a laboratory in which the affirmations were proved and from which spiritually motivated findings were being shared with everyone who wanted or needed them.

There was something else. In the traditional church we ministers were on a salary, as concerned about being paid as was any worker in any other profession. We had a scripture text to justify our view, "The laborer is worthy of his hire." We wanted to live in circumstances commensurate with those of our parishioners.

Unity gave an impression of a new approach. It presented a new image. Charles and Myrtle Fillmore asked nothing for themselves, wanted nothing for themselves, nothing more than the wherewithal to meet their modest needs. People visiting the Tracy Avenue headquarters saw the teeming office from which the nation-wide ministry was conducted. They sauntered through the unpretentious home where the Fillmores lived. They got the feeling of self-sacrifice and dedication all the way from custodian to comptroller. They went away believing that God was in charge and that good was being manifested.

That is how early Unity impressed itself on me. Prosperity was not a matter of money. It was, as has been said, a matter of the spirit of man recognizing itself as the spirit of God working His will with "substance," according to the light of truth.

Questions that had annoyed me in my pastorate: how to raise money without being accused of commercialism, how to advance the work of the church without falling victim to the taint of promotionalism, how to deal with money and how far money should be permitted to deal with me; these Unity answered with a single phrase, "Religion is God's business in the world and you are His partner in this business."

Charles and Myrtle Fillmore believed it and lived it, Mother Fillmore agreed with it, and Lowell and Rick were more and more overwhelmed with it. Unity was working in a family's life in a most remarkable way. Once when a member of the staff told Papa Charley that Unity had a slight surplus in the bank, he exclaimed, "Well, we must get rid of that!" And he did. He used it for expanding the work, which meant helping out someone in need.

On another occasion he asked his secretary to make out a check for $175 for a person in financial straits. She said, "We don't have that much in the account." "Well," he said, "make out the check and hold it until we do, then give it to him."

It was a matter of outlook and a point of view. I learned from Unity that as long as I considered money an affront to God, that is what it was. My consciousness made it an affront until I became aware of the fact that money is an extension of creativity, an evidence of substance spiritualized. I may still have clung to my stubborn insistence that money was the root of evil and that the pursuit of it has led men into the deepest sins, but I now understood a bit better that the attitude toward it determines the role it plays in life. In his moments of deepest reflection every man knows how he stands in relation to money, whether he is the master of it or whether it masters him.

That was how Unity approached the situation. Whenever anyone asked, "What shall I do about money? How much shall I tithe? What shall I give and what shall I keep?" Unity answered, "We will pray. You make the decision."

There were financial growing pains during Unity's fledgling years and the Fillmores, too, were often criticized. Vituperators on the outside accused them of supplementing the working of Divine law with promotional ingenuity typically Americanesque. Was this a just criticism? It depended upon your point of view or, more correctly, upon the Unity point of view.

Revenue from such sources as the sale of a pin bearing an emblem of Unity's Winged-Globe, the sale of souvenir china plates, and the program which distributed crisp, new dollar bills to those who would agree to use them as a catalyst for demonstrating prosperity faith were negligible. As to the latter, some two thousand bills were distributed; some five thousand were returned. These experiments during the early years of Unity were part of its promotional experimentation, though this may not excuse the methods or justify them.

The prosperity-oriented consciousness of Charles Fillmore was persuaded beyond the shadow of a doubt that God was an all-providing and an all-supplying Father blessing all who willingly adventured in the realm of faith. "It is our right," he contended, "to be prosperous," and added to this the paramount goal of his lifework, "It is ours to set up on earth the kingdom of the heavens."

He was often misunderstood, this man who worked as though the kingdom depended upon him. He was often misrepresented, this man who in the early days of Unity lugged the heavy rolls of printing paper on his shoulders through Kansas City streets. He was often criticized, this man who made God an intimate partner in his life, who talked with Him as one talks with an old friend, and who listened to Him as one listens to a beloved teacher.

But those who knew him and who found within themselves a deepened faith and a new version of life because of him, they not only understood, they faithfully followed his prescription for prosperity: *Recognize—Affirm—Translate—Give thanks.* And in so doing they earnestly employed his affirmations:

"I trust God's universal law of prosperity in all my affairs."

"Infinite wisdom guides me, divine love prospers me, and I am successful in everything I undertake."

Needless to say, Charles Fillmore was a forerunner of the power of positive thinking in our contemporary religious life. He launched a cycle of affirmative faith which carried in its wake Protestant and Catholic leaders alike, some of whom in later days were to acknowledge their debt to him and recommend his statements to their followers, statements such as,

"I am not fearful of poverty, and I am under obligations to no one. My opulent Father has poured out to me all resources, and I am a mighty channel of abundance."

"I am always provided for because I have faith in God as my infinite source of supply."

"Father, I thank Thee for unlimited increase in mind, money, and affairs."

Though these affirmations were widely accepted by non-Unity people, some of the writings of Charles Fillmore were not accepted, particularly his parody on the Twenty-third Psalm,

"The Lord is my banker; my credit is good.
He maketh me to lie down in the consciousness of omnipresent abundance;
He giveth me the key to His strongbox.

He restoreth my faith in His riches;
He guideth me in the paths of prosperity for His name's sake.
Yea, though I walk in the very shadow of debt,
I shall fear no evil, for Thou art with me;
Thy silver and Thy gold, they secure me.
Thou preparest a way for me in the presence of the collector;
Thou fillest my wallet with plenty; my measure runneth over.
Surely goodness and plenty will follow me all the days of
    my life;
And I shall do business in the name of the Lord forever."

Some Christians were shocked. Especially those who could not see the twinkle in his eyes and who did not know of his profound love for the Psalm as David had sung it. Incidentally, my father, a businessman, thought it quite wonderful. My mother, who had started reading Unity's *Daily Word*, declared she would have to reserve judgment.

What Fillmore sought to do in his "Psalm" was to deal with one of man's deepest concerns, insecurity; and to set in bold perspective one of man's secret sources of worry, money. He wanted to remind men of their never-failing access to the Giver of every good and perfect gift. He wanted to impress men with the fact that there was no separating life into categories of the material and the spiritual. He hoped to make it clear that there was no such thing as a Sunday religion and a religion of the workaday world.

"Some people," he said, "think of prosperity as something separate from their spiritual experience. They live in two worlds: in one for six days of the week when man runs things, and in the other on the seventh day when God is given a chance to show what He can do. Do all things to the glory of God seven days a week rather than one. Take God into all your affairs!"

Recognize—Affirm—Translate—Give thanks.

With this prosperity prescription, my philosophy about money began to take shape, my feeling about money began to change, my attitude toward money was altered. Money was God's substance materialized and those who caught on found this to be miraculously true.

As for the Unity movement, it prospered even in the dismal days of the thirties. Although the Tracy Avenue buildings which covered a city block remained as the headquarters, work had started on the acres which now comprise Unity Village. As early as the summer of 1928 Unity followers from all over the world came to bless the first Village buildings: Silent Unity and the Unity Tower. They came 300 strong and lived in tents on the dedicated acres, acres where, on my Thursday at Unity, the rain came down. God's rain. This, too, seemed as it should be, for in the record of the 1928 meeting, it is reported that it rained for eight straight days. For a week-and-a-day the 100 canvas tents stood wet and soggy under the murky skies. Delegates sloshed through the mud, slept in the damp, listened to the beat of the rain on the pools of water in the barren site, and built duck walks to the Silent Unity building.

Knowing Unity people I have no doubt that the delegates counted it all as being in divine order. Knowing Charles Fillmore, I am confident that his faith was never shaken or that he failed to see the sunlight already shining on the Unity that was still to be.

It was during the depression years that he published his famous book, *Prosperity*. As far as Fillmore was concerned, the so-called "lean years" were a perversion of truth. In the midst of want he gave thanks for plenty. In the time of seeming setback in the building plans at the "Farm," as Unity Village was called, he voiced his confident affirmations. Depression-beaten men turned to Unity then, turned to it as the physically sick turned to it, seeking health and help. *Prosperity* was a hopeful book, a book whose 200 pages bristled with confidence in God's bounty and hailed the glory of the Jesus way, which taught that, "Divine Mind is the one and only reality."

That is how Fillmore began the book, explaining at once that, though he had titled it *Prosperity*, it should be borne in mind that "In the coming commerce man will not be a slave to money. Humanity's needs will be met in ways that are not now thought practical. We shall serve for the joy of serving and prosperity will flow to us and through us in streams of plenty."

He was never to abandon the hope of utopia. Men said he would never reach it, but he found it in reaching *for* it. It was a spiritual quest and money was but a by-product.

However, *Prosperity* had a great deal to say about money and the use of money and the way to get money, and Unity followers bought the book eagerly—and so did I. No one needed it more than I and although I may not have demonstrated its propositions as productively as did others, I nonetheless benefited phenomenally from the merit of the Fillmore premises.

They helped me get rid of a sense of lack and limitation on God's part. I grew up with the belief that God's good was measurable, like grain in a bin, and that there was just so much grain to go around. More than that, I had it fixed in my mind that each man had been given a scoop of a certain size, and that mine was just big enough or small enough to help me "get by" in this highly competitive world. Now I took a long leap toward a new belief. God's resources are *unlimited*. I had *not* arbitrarily been given a scoop of a certain size. My capacity for prosperity in its various forms— talent, money, productivity—was also unlimited. God's substance did not fluctuate with the times. It did not decrease during depressions and rise when the market went up. God's resources were ever the same; constant, abundant, freely circulating, available to all.

Furthermore, I realized as I never had before that, "Money is the materialization of ideas." This principle shifted my sporadic views about prosperity into a semblance, at least, of stabilized thinking.

"The possessions of the Father," Fillmore proclaimed, "are not in stocks and bonds, but in the divine possibilities implanted in the mind and soul of every man. Through the mind of man, ideas are brought into being. Through the soul of man God's wealth of love finds its expression. It is well said that the mind is the crucible in which the ideal is transmuted into the real."

With this realization, ideas became synonymous with the coin of the realm. To rightly assess one's prosperity, it was necessary to take an inventory of the ideas stored in consciousness. The total wealth of life was therefore already ours, needing only the manifestation of the ideal into the real.

The power of affirmations lay in the fact that they trained the subconscious to react to the realization of the goal affirmed. When I proclaimed, "I have faith in the substance of God working in and through me to increase and bring abundance into my world," my faith started to work in the mind substance and make me prosperous. Prosperity meant work, but not in the frantic, frenzied whir of life. It meant work first of all in the tranquil world of ideas which is ever ready and waiting to help us receive what we rightly claim as our own.

This "right to claim" was one of the most helpful of all hints in my upward climb toward a new belief. It carried me over many a deep-seated preoccupation which had long been a part of my nature. For example, I had always been tempted to depend upon others for my security. I always hoped that someday someone would come along and subsidize me or underwrite or finance me, though why or for what reason was never quite clear. I didn't actually subscribe to the concept, "The world owes me a living," but I certainly dreamed about it.

Prosperity diagnosed my condition in bold, black print when it said, "The other fellow's realization of substance will not guarantee your supply. You must become conscious of it for *yourself*. Identify *yourself* with substance until you make it yours; it will change your finances, destroy your fears, stop your worries, and you will soon begin to rejoice in the ever-present bounty of God."

The words were for me. They were a finger singling me out of the vast reading audience. The statement was something more. It was an epitaph over a self that I was bound and determined to make short shrift of once and for all. And I did. I recognized *substance*. I *recognized* that there is no lack and I recognized that the law of cause and effect operates interdependently in all of life. I *affirmed* thoughts of abundance in the assurance that these thoughts are irrevocably true and workable for me. I *translated* the thoughts into action. I *gave thanks* for the demonstration of truth. And the moment I followed this formula, everyone, it seemed, wanted to do something for me!

It was a great leap and one that I was eager to recommend to others. I wanted to say, as Fillmore had said, "Be still and turn within to the great source. See with the eye of faith that the whole world is filled with substance. See it falling all about you as snowflakes of gold and silver and affirm with assurance: I have unbounded faith in the all-present spiritual substance increasing and multiplying at my word."

I had always liked the phrase, "falling about you as snow-flakes of gold and silver." But on this Thursday I was more inclined to say, "falling about you like rain."

God's rain.

In true metaphysical fashion, Fillmore saw prosperity lessons subtly tucked away within the casual sayings of Scripture. Take, for example, the Parable of the Prodigal Son. The Far Away Country where the runaway youth dissipated his inheritance was, according to Fillmore, a land where the divine law of plenty was not recognized. The "inheritance" was metaphysically interpreted as "knowledge of truth." The father, to whom the prodigal returned, represented the God-mind. The robe with which he was clothed, was an object lesson in good apparel for body and soul; the gold ring, a symbol of unlimited means; the shoes, a new understanding of earthly conditions; and the feast, with its fatted calf, was the assurance that God does not dole out a stingy ration, but showers with universal abundance and prosperity all those who return to Him in truth.

To metaphysician Fillmore the six days of creation symbolically set forth the six steps involved in bringing an idea into manifestation.

1. "Let there be light," means "let there be understanding." This is the principle of recognition, the recognition that God will provide, has indeed already provided the one universal substance.

2. "Let there be a firmament," is to be interpreted as a "firm place in the mind, a dividing of the true from the apparent."

3. "Let the land appear," is a way of saying that we should visualize clearly what it is we need and bring the concept up out of the waters of doubt. This is the principle of "affirming."

4. "Let there be lights in the firmament of the heaven," means metaphysically, "Let there be clarity and recognition of the law of increase."

5. "Let the waters bring forth abundantly," refers to the "translating" factor, or, as Fillmore says, "the thought of lack penetrated and so charged with the truth of God's omnipresent abundance that all consciousness of lack and poverty disappear."

6. "Let us make man in our image," symbolizes the full recognition of our oneness with God and the birth of the divine idea, the perfect man, the Christ, brought forth on the sixth day.

7. "And God rested and blessed the seventh day and sanctified it," means that the final principle of our prosperity prescription is enunciated in "Giving thanks" and resting in the knowledge of truth. *Relax, let go, let God*

Many other scripture lessons are interpreted by Unity as prosperity patterns. In the 4th chapter of Second Kings the widow who complained to Elisha that the creditor was coming to take her two sons as bondmen typified a person who has lost consciousness of God's supply, the sons represent the thoughts of debt, the prophet is divine understanding, the house is the body consciousness, and the pot of oil is faith in spiritual substance.

The neighbors in the story were, according to Unity, negative thoughts and their empty vessels were symbols of lack. To "shut the door," as the widow was told to do, meant to enter the inner consciousness and shut out thoughts of poverty. "Pouring" the oil into all the places that were empty was the demonstration of how faith fills every obligation until every debt is paid.

The symbolical promise of the windows of heaven being opened for those who bring their tithes into the storehouse means that the mind (heaven) is filled to overflowing with creative and productive ideas. Tithing, according to Unity, means more than merely putting a tenth of one's earnings to work for the Lord; it means recognizing that all of one's money, possessions, talent, love, and time are God's substance over which we are stewards for a while. Such are the ingredients in the prosperity ideal. Such are the goals toward which the consecrated life must strive and that is why the student of truth must be bold enough to affirm, "I claim the

will of God for me to be rich, prosperous, and successful!"
Recognize—Affirm—Translate—Give thanks.

The time came in 1949 when trucks and moving vans formed a cavalcade to the site near Lee's Summit, Missouri, new address of the Unity movement. Piecemeal moving had been going on for a long time, but now it became thorough and complete. The Tracy Avenue Building was taken over as the offices for the Kansas City chapter of the Salvation Army. Unity Farm became Unity headquarters, home of Silent Unity, training school for Unity students, offices of Silent-70, editorial and publishing rooms for Unity publications, retreat grounds for seekers of truth, and inspirational center for a questing world.

Today Unity Village is all this and more. It is in itself an object lesson in prosperity. It grew and prospered because it *Recognized* that the law of cause and effect operates interdependently in all of life; it *Affirmed* thoughts of abundance in the assurance that these thoughts are irrevocably true and workable. It *Translated* the thoughts into action. It *Gave thanks* for the demonstration of truth.

As I walked and visited in Unity Village on this rainy Thursday, I appreciated more than ever what I had learned about prosperity from Unity teaching. This appreciation came easily, just by thinking, just by remembering. Actually, just by listening to the rain.

God's rain.

CHAPTER SEVEN

How Unity Heals
the Sick

Among the mail forwarded to me during my stay at Unity Village was a letter which said, "Our son Stephen has shown remarkable improvement in the last two months. Our prayers and the prayers of those who have prayed with us have been answered. It is only now that we begin to realize how much a strong faith in the power of God has meant and means to us. This was particularly significant for us all through the Lenten season. Silent Unity gave us an inspiring prayer: You Are God's Whole and Perfect Child. Every Cell in Your Body Is Aglow with His Light, Life, and Love. Thank you for helping us along a very difficult road."

Stephen's case had been diagnosed by physicians as leukemia. I had heard the story from the boy's father, an engineering professor on a western university campus. There had been the customary clinical consultations, the shock of the diagnosis, the need for conveying the report to Stephen's mother, the grief and frustration, then the anxiety and gloom which struck the household.

The parents' question was the inevitable, "Why?" Why should an eleven-year-old boy, a quiet, religiously minded boy, be stricken with this seemingly incurable disease? The attitude of the parents was typical of those who from childhood have been urged and warned to trust in God. Now in their attempt to understand this tragedy, they saw God through a glass more dark than even the Scripture had foretold.

What kind of a God? A God who meted out justice? Then what had Stephen done to warrant this "justice"? A God of mercy? Then why this inexorable medical pronouncement? "Your boy has eight months or a year to live," they were told. Why? This was the cry with which the father and mother stormed the implacable wall which countless others, under similar circumstances have frenziedly assailed.

It was then I told the father about Unity, particularly Silent Unity, saying I was convinced that Unity records and my Unity research bore out the fact that spiritual healing is a reality in Unity work. I was as sure of this as I was sure of "miracles" generally, for in my years of delving into the mystery of this field, all the way from the grotto at Lourdes to the tent meetings of faith healers, I had found too many testimonies and too much evidence to write off these cures as fiction, as medical remissions, or as psychosomatic *vorstellung* or illusion.

I tried to explain to Stephen's father that healing miracles, though they might be beyond the ordinary course of events, were never beyond the laws of nature or Divine Law, and that the miraculous must be adjudged in ratio to the degree in which these laws are understood. It is not tautological to say that miracles are for those who believe in them, for this is actually part of the process.

Spiritual healing, I contended, is for those who have the necessary capacity for faith or who can demonstrate the necessary will to believe. It is for those wise men of God, fools often in the eyes of the world who with steady, solid steps walk *free from fear*, and this may be the greatest miracle of all. Which brings us to Unity.

Unity says, I Am Made in the Image and Likeness of God. My Body Expresses His Perfection in Every Detail.

Repeat this, believing. Repeat this, accepting it as truth. Repeat this in the confidence that nothing can deter you, and you will find that you are first of all casting out fear. Sickness, evil, the devil in his many forms, are not entities in Unity as they are in many religions. They are errors in the understanding of truth. They are fear factors and must be denied.

Denials are a unique part of Unity's healing process. Charles Fillmore usually prescribed them as a prologue to the use of affirmations. He said they should be made as if you were gently sweeping away cobwebs from the mind. Designed to get rid of the dust of doubt and fear, denials in Unity are a method of driving out any pernicious illusion which may be blocking the path of healing.

"I deny the belief that I have inherited disease, sickness, ignorance, or any mental limitation!" That is a popular Unity denial and it is to be stated with the power and conviction of an affirmation.

"I deny the belief that I am a child of the flesh and that I must suffer the sins of my forefathers unto the third and fourth generation." That is a denial open to criticism by the traditional church, but strongly defended by Fillmore as being against the law of truth.

"I deny that I have inherited the consequences of fear from my ancestors, or that the race can reflect its fears upon me."

This denial reminded me that I had to deny the fact that I inherited migraine headaches from my mother, a belief that had haunted me for many years! It was commonplace in my home for me to be told, "You come by your headaches naturally. Your mother has them and you are bound to have them, too." I was also assured that it was natural that I should lose my hair because my father had lost his. I still cannot understand why my brothers did not lose theirs, since they were as much their father's sons as I. Did they, I wonder, deny the thought, while I believed it?

"Deny!" says Unity. Clear away the cobwebs. Get rid of the dust. Make straight the way so that the Great Physician can do His work, for it is He who does the healing. Invoke His presence with the Lord's prayer. Talk to Him as though He were present. "The first move in all healing," Unity suggests, "is the recognition on the part of the healer and on the part of the patient that God is present as an all-powerful mind."

In Unity, spiritual healing is not merely a real cure for imaginary diseases or an imaginary cure for real diseases; it is the fulfillment of the working of a Law by those conversant with the Law.

Actually it is more than a law. It is a divine principle at the heart of which is the reference just made: *freedom from fear*. Healing is in direct proportion to the degree in which healer and patient can remove fear from patient and healer. Both Unity's denials and affirmations are directed toward effecting this consciousness. Drive out the deep-seated, subconscious fear by affirming that: My Trust Is in God, I Am Not Afraid. His All-Wise, All-Loving, All-Adjusting Power Fills Me with Enduring Health and Strength.

Unity seeks to banish anxiety with the unshaken conviction that: God Wants Me To Be Well So That I Can More Perfectly Do His Will.

It rids the patient of his lurking sense of guilt, his misplaced contention that healing is not for him, by urging him to affirm: Health Is the Normal Condition of Man. Health Is a Condition True To the Reality of My Being. This is one of Unity's strongest healing affirmations, for it assures the individual that *nature* is always on his side. *God* is always on his side. *Good* is always on his side.

A woman afflicted with an eye injury was greatly helped by the assurance that the *eye wills to be well*. She had always believed that every cell and fibre of the body wills to be well, but the eye, she thought, was something different. The eye, she supposed, was given to deterioration instead of healing, and when this assumption was dispelled and she accepted the truth that the nature of the eye is health, she found an aid in dispelling the fear that the eye would not heal.

There are Unity members who diligently perform eye exercises, believing that the eyes can be strengthened through proper care and diet and by means of specific techniques such as palming, blinking, gently sun-bathing the eyes, and other practices which can be found in books in this specific field. All spiritual healers are slightly frustrated when they make claims for all sorts of cures and then find that they are helpless when it comes to presbyopia! Many have been the times that I have had healers of one type or another speak to my students about marvelous healings and the limitlessness of faith, only to be faced with the persistent question, "Why do you wear glasses?"

Unity members also wear glasses, but within Unity's ranks are individuals who improve their eyesight with determined disciplines and who effectively put off wearing glasses with the affirmation, "I Deny All Belief in Failing Eyesight. My Eyes Are the Eyes of Spirit, Strong, Youthful, Clear Sighted and Perfect."

That is how Unity heals.

It heals by turning the table on disease.

In the face of a rash of ads that warn us that we must accept at least two sick spells per year and in defiance of the TV medicine men who fill the hearts and homes of Americans with the consciousness that the flu is out to get you and that colds are here to stay, Unity stands up to affirm: I Do Not Believe in Colds, Weakness, Inefficiency, or Negativeness of Any Kind. I Am a Strong, Bold, Fearless, Free Spirit, and I Am Filled with the Energy, Vigor, and Vitality of Omnipresent, Omnipotent Life.

Given time, right thinking may even do away with the common cold!

But whether it does or not, Unity continues to broadcast

its unswerving conviction that Harmony Is Health, and Health Is Harmony.

It sets the law of healing into operation through the recognition that Your Life Is God's Life.

It draws unto itself the breath of life by insisting: I Freely, Steadily Breathe the Vital Essence of God's Life and by His Life I Am Perfectly Healed.

No wonder, then, that it said to Stephen's parents and to the boy: You Are God's Whole and Perfect Child. Every Cell in Your Body Is Aglow with His Light, Life, and Love.

In all of which Unity does not deny the fact of sickness. *Truth* it might not have been, this leukemia, but *fact* it surely was. Unity does not deny the fact of sickness any more than it denies darkness, but it knows that if you approach darkness realistically with light, it will be shown that darkness is but an absence of light, as sickness is an absence of health. In this way Unity is a study of the true nature of things, and believes that it is God's good will to "demonstrate over sickness."

The Bible has its own evidence for the working of this principle. Once a sightless man groped his way through Palestine streets and those who watched him wondered why he was blind. They surmised that God was punishing him for some hidden sin or victimizing him because of the transgressions of his parents. When an itinerant Teacher came that way, someone called out to Him, "Tell us, why is this man blind? Who sinned, he or his parents, that he was born blind?" To which the Teacher said, "Neither hath this man sinned nor his parents; but that the works of God should be manifest in him." And the Teacher healed him.

Among the miracles of Jesus few are more descriptive of Unity's approach to healing. It cannot be said too often: *you must get rid of the fear that God is a wrathful God.* You must get rid of the anxiety that God is a merciless God. You must deny the mistaken and deeply ingrained apprehension that you are the victim of a capricious and wanton Creator who delights in afflicting the children of men. In the deepest moment of despair you must hear the words: You Are God's Whole and Perfect Child. Every Cell in Your Body Is Aglow with His Light, Life, and Love.

There is something besides fear that holds back healing. It is the age-old doctrine that men are destined to suffer along the way of life, that it has all always been this way and will continue so to be. Here, again, Unity boldly denies this supposition. But it is ready to admit that suffering exists and most Unity students will agree that suffering may have meaning. In fact, they admit that the quest for healing may be the path for a new discovery of God.

The quest for healing may cause some men to analyze their habits and their life to see whether they are in harmony with God. Suffering may give an individual a new perspective on his sense of values. It may offer an insight into one's deeper hidden responses, hidden so deeply that only the blunt key of sudden misfortune may be able to open the door. Suffering may fulfill something in life as vital and needful as that fulfilled through joy. In fact, each is sharpened by the other, and each has its own revelation.

But having admitted all this and agreed to this, Unity approaches sickness, suffering and disease with the basic assurance that God will not willfully tempt His children with evil, nor annoy His children with pain, nor terrorize His children with tragedy. Unity teaches that though suffering and sickness may be common to men, they are not inevitable.

Most people, however, have been so saturated with the belief that suffering is part of God's will that they cannot visualize a world or an individual without it. This is the dust cloud floating around many persons who seek spiritual healing. Unity may assure them that he who is master of his faith is master of his health, but all too often both religion

and medicine will not let us forget that suffering is universal and that sickness is as much a part of every life as is
death.

Charles Fillmore said of these ideas that "they have one
argument which they always use to impress us, that of the
fear of results if we should dare to come out and meet them
in open opposition. This fear of opposing ideas, even when
we know them to be wrong, seems to be woven into our
very mental fabric. This fear is symbolized by the spear of
Goliath which, as the story relates, was like a weaver's
beam."

The historic churches have been especially active in
deifying suffering. They have continually called upon men
to remember the Proverb, "My son, despise not the chastening of the Lord," and promoted the literal interpretation of
the Psalmist who said, "I know that Thy judgments are
right, and that Thou in faithfulness hath afflicted me."
Young people have been catechized with the familiar text,
"Whom the Lord loveth He chasteneth." These words always disturbed me because I wondered why, if the chastening was of the Lord and if it truly was an act of love, why
we should not calmly submit and ride it out, as it were. No
one seemed to do this; not even the most religious of my
friends. I found very few bending under this chastening. At
the slightest sign of sickness among the faithful, doctors
were summoned and specialists were called and every material means at man's disposal were rallied to fight against
the Lord's decree.

When medical men came to answer the call, they corrob-
orated what the clergy had proposed. Sickness, they
agreed, was universal and there was no escaping the fact
that disease, like death, was inevitable. Soon they supplied
us with statistics. One out of every five, we were warned,
could expect to be a cancer victim. One out of every six was
ripe for tuberculosis. One out of every seven would be a

casualty to muscular dystrophy. One member of every family could expect to spend one week annually in a hospital.

The statistics helped make it all come to pass, as statistics always do when enough people fix them irrevocably in their mind. Hospitals to meet the statistics were feverishly built and billboards helped frighten the public into meeting the prognostications. The drug industry became one of the largest and most aggressive cartels in the land. The individual, inundated by pressure from preacher to pharmaceutical expert, did not have a chance. He finally gave up, persuaded that he would have to learn to live with sickness and disease as he was learning to live with war and man's inability ever to effect a lasting peace.

Outside of the wilderness cry of itinerant spiritual healers, one of the first modern voices to speak out against the inevitability and deification of suffering was the group known collectively as Christian Science. Today we commonly associate the term with the Church of Christ, Scientist, but in the period when Unity was young, Christian Science was a generic term used by numerous aggregations of metaphysical healers.

Charles Fillmore, although among the first to credit Mary Baker Eddy with giving the greatest impetus to all that Christian Science implied, made it clear that when he used the term Christian Science he meant "the many schools of metaphysical thought sailing under the general name." The Fillmores had studied the teachings of Mrs. Eddy and practiced them, as they had studied and practiced other expressions of Truth in this general field, all the way from the Pythagorian school and the esoteric teachings of Hermes Trismegistus, to Paracelsus and Richard M. Bucke.

Unlike Mrs. Eddy, the Fillmores could not accept suffering as an illusion or look upon pain as a figment of mortal mind. They knew the "reality" of the world of the sick. They had experienced it. They knew that millions lay daily in hospital beds, that millions were confined to their homes, and that other millions throughout the world despaired of ever again knowing the meaning of good health or a buoyant life.

The Fillmores knew this world and I in my work of religious research was continually besieged by letters from people who were searching desperately for cures, who had loved ones who needed help in the field of healing, and who, having sought healing in the myriad paths of medicine wanted to know if there did not exist somewhere, somehow, a "miracle worker" who, like the Christ, walked through this world with healing in his hands.

It was a serious world, this world of the sick, much more serious than was realized by those who were well. To many it was a world unknown, excepting for brief occasions when, for one reason or another, they were momentarily involved in its contingencies.

I, too, had often wondered about the "miracle workers." Like the Fillmores, I had found many men in the medical profession who bore such greatness of stature, such courage and skill that their importance in the field of healing could not be denied. Who could overlook the work of a Schweitzer in Africa, a Mellon in Haiti, a Dooley in Laos, or a Seagrave in Burma, or who would question the importance of the physician in one's home town whose selfless service had saved many a life and relieved many a pain?

There is nothing in Unity that forbids a person going to a doctor. Unity believes that God works through medicine and through medical and non-medical professions which are dedicated to healing. The question as to where one should draw the line between medical aid and full and complete reliance on divine healing is not clearly resolved in Unity. Every minister, in fact, every Unity affiliate must make his own decision as to where God's will ends and man's skills begin. Some Unity teachers settle the problem by saying, "You cannot draw these fine lines. All is God and God is all."

Then the knotty question arises, "What about inoculations, cold shots, miracle drugs, and the like?" And what about one's dependence upon so-called preventive medicine? Does such dependence water down one's faith in God? Is God in the penicillin and in the cortisone and in the sleeping tablet? Unity says, "You must decide. You must listen to your guidance. You must live and act in accordance with your highest consciousness in the matter."

I have found, however, that Unity quite agrees that unless we get at the true cause of our dilemmas through a spiritual analysis we are making concessions to our weakness. Every time we take an aspirin without analyzing why we have the headache, we have slipped back a step in our conquest of self.

In the case of Charles and Myrtle Fillmore we find that their reliance upon the Great Physician ruled out reliance upon anything less than God. They developed such confidence in the reality of the indwelling Christ, such complete faith in the "Kingdom within" that there was no room for anything but "God's good."

Once, even a qualified physician commended the scope of this faith. When Papa Charley lay in pain following an automobile accident, the doctor who had treated the other injured people came to where he lay. He stooped down to give medical assistance, but Fillmore said, "Leave me alone, please. I will do this in my own way."

"There," said the doctor quietly, "is a man."

There, in fact, was more than a man. There was the spirit of faith which for this particular individual was all sufficient. What was Charles Fillmore's spiritual orientation as he lay there? What was he thinking? How was he dispelling the fear that he might not ever recover from this injury? What affirmation was he holding to as he visualized himself unharmed and well? Undoubtedly, it was the prayer given to the boy Stephen, "You are God's whole and perfect child. Every cell in your body is aglow with His light, life, and love."

Lying there, he beheld himself, not chastened, but healed by the power and love of God in whose light Charles Fillmore saw himself as perfect man.

That is how Unity heals.

Actor John Payne told me about his automobile accident in New York City. He had just stepped into the street when a careening car struck him with such force that he was tossed up through the windshield and thrown back to the curb. His scalp was badly cut, his face was lacerated, bits of glass had lodged in his eyes, and one leg was shattered. As he lay in a pool of blood, he found himself overwhelmingly strengthened by what he referred to as "the truth of Unity teachings."

Affirmations passed through his mind, sustaining him. In a most remarkable way he *knew* that "life, strength, and intelligence of Spirit" were active in his body and that he had nothing to fear as long as this thought of divine order remained established in his consciousness.

Among the first to rush to his side was a youngster whom Payne managed to ask if he happened to know a certain man living in this busy block. The boy responded by saying that he knew the man well because he had often made deliveries at his apartment. So the youngster dashed off with the message and as John Payne lay there, he was more persuaded than ever that this was more than just coincidence. God was at work. The harmonizing, healing, adjusting power of God was taking over and all would be well.

All was well although there were those who despaired that actor Payne would live and there were others who were confident he would be too disfigured ever to act again. They did not know the power of prayers issuing from Unity circles, and the power of God working through the hands of skilled surgeons. A chain of healing was established which ran all the way from New York to California and when I spoke to Mr. Payne I would never have known that the accident had ever happened to him, excepting that his faith was so tremendously secure.

That is how Unity heals.

Why does it work with some people and not with others? It is, I think, dependent, as I have said, upon the degree of faith. It is related in a very real way to intuition, that inner knowing which is beyond outer reasoning. Some individuals simply *know* how free they are from fear, how near they are to God, and more particularly, how near God is to them. They know, though they could never articulate the knowing. Behind the affirmation is the philosophy; behind the philosophy the will to believe; behind the will to believe is the *knowing*.

That is how Unity heals.

Unity heals by the unequivocal belief that health is man's heritage, that nature is remedial, that the mind is therapeutic, and that the God-spirit in man is a perfect spirit.

In Unity, all healing is divine healing. There is no conflict between science and religion where each is built upon and involved in Truth. Unity admonishes the individual that if he puts himself into the doctor's hands, he should have confidence in the doctor and cooperate with him. If a patient harbors antagonistic feelings against the doctor he may block the course of healing. Medicine, according to metaphysical teaching, is not merely a substance which produces a chemical reaction, it is a thought-complex which effects results according to the relationship prevailing between the mind of the physician, the patient, and all who are involved in the healing process.

One of the most spectacular cases in which the harmony of this Unity approach was demonstrated came to my attention in St. Petersburg, Florida, when I sat with a man at a supper table. A photographer approached us with the request that he wished to take a flashlight picture. To this my companion responded somewhat whimsically, "If you are going to do that, I had better cover my eye."

When I asked him the reason for this remark, he said, "Well, you know, my one eye is a glass eye and the light could rebound into the film!" He covered his eye and the picture was taken.

"A glass eye?" I asked after the photographer had gone. "I have been with you for an hour or more and I must say that I would never have noticed."

"Yes," he reflected, "it was a good job."

Then he told me of how he had gone one day to inspect some road work for the city of St. Petersburg. As he stepped down into a pit, the iron clam-shovel, operated by a crane, swung around and caught his head, crushing his face in its fearful vice-like motion, lifting him from the ground and then dropping him into the pool of blood that gushed from his eyes and mouth. His mangled features, one eye torn from its socket, his seemingly lifeless body, made even the possibility of moving him to a stretcher or into an ambulance seem utterly futile. Nonetheless, he was taken to a hospital.

By this time, his wife had been notified and she in turn had called the Unity minister, Unity workers, and Silent Unity. Now she stood with the doctors during their consultation. At one point she said to the Unity minister, "I am grateful we have the best physicians possible here." The Unity minister replied, "God, the great physician, is also here." The wife took her husband's hand and to the apparently unconscious form she kept repeating Unity affirmations.

In relating the story, this man said that as he lay there the words filled him with a sense of light and love. In his mind was a vision of God helping and healing, and he had no fear or doubt from that moment that he would live. Unity prayers sustained the skilled hands of the surgeons who contributed to this man's remarkable recovery. Unity affirmations gave him strength. Unity's "believability" was so strong that even today you feel it when you are with this man. His face shows few scars, but there is even less of a scar in his heart for circumstances against which he might bear untold resentment and bitterness as far as his accident was concerned.

Maybe there will always be accidents and suffering in the world, but with such faith in the good there is a chance, at least, that the world will grow toward goodness and truth. Unity affirms that he who sees the invisible can do the impossible, and that, too, is how Unity heals. It heals by meeting situations with the interminable confidence that there is no limit to God's power.

You Are God's Whole and Perfect Child. Every Cell in Your Body Is Aglow with His Light, Life, and Love.

For developing the proper attitude toward necessary surgery and for bringing the full force of healing faith to those who undergo hospitalization, Unity has prepared a most helpful booklet titled, *You Are Not Alone*. Its 33 pages are spontaneous in their insight into the patient's mind, and I doubt whether more helpful material can be found than these affirmations, techniqes, and inspirational hints for health. Several lines, titled *Realization*, by Florence Taylor, perfectly express the Unity approach:

> I *can* be healed. God's own life-giving power
> Flows freely through my body hour by hour.
>
> I *must* be healed so that I may express
> My Father's love and joy and perfectness.
>
> I *will* be healed; for this my aim shall be,
> To let God's perfect will be done in me.
>
> I *am* healed now; for just as God sees me,
> I see myself: harmonious, fearless, free.

There are endless healing affirmations in the Unity arsenal. Many were composed by the Fillmores, others were inspired by Unity students, some grew spontaneously out of areas of need as Unity ministers went about their pastoral duties. Many are born out of the silence of Silent Unity or are submitted anonymously by individuals who have had some extraordinary healing experience.

The sayings of the Christ and the promises of Scripture are the rich soil from which the affirmations have grown. "Be ye transformed by the renewing of your mind" is at the heart of many a healing phrase. "Let the mind which dwelled in Christ Jesus dwell abundantly in you" has suggested such affirmations as, God, Mighty in the Midst of Me, Is Healing My Body, Guiding Me On My Way, Revealing Himself to Me As My Help in Every Need, and Divine Order Is Now Established in My Mind, Body, and Affairs by the Power of the Indwelling Christ.

"I, the Lord, healeth thee," gives rise to such affirmations as God Is My Strength and My Peace: My Heart Has Faith in Him. The Angel of His Presence Guides and Guards Me.

"Beloved, now are ye the sons of God," inspires a Unity member to say, I Am the Illumined Child of God, Filled with the Spirit of Divine Love and Wisdom, by Which I Am Guided in All My Ways, and Led into That Which Is for My Highest Good.

In short, every constructive scripture text is a usable affirmation and can be transposed into a contemporary maxim which works for good. Hear the words, "I am the Light of the World" and you can establish them in your life by affirming, "I Am Radiant with the Light of God!"

Unity's prayer-poems also have their healing credentials wherever Unity has gone. A young minister confided to me that the very first time he was called upon to pray for a desperately sick member of his congregation, he could think of no more effective words than the Prayer of Protection which begins, "The light of God surrounds me . . ."

One of my earliest investigations of so-called healing miracles in Unity revealed that the Prayer of Faith had been the affirmation that brought recovery. A woman living in a Mississippi River town had been seized by the frightening realization that she was "slowly paralyzing." The feeling of "something holding me back" haunted her and sent her to a Minnesota hospital where her condition was diagnosed as multiple sclerosis. In her late twenties, she was adjusting herself to the role of an invalid, and her orthodox minister said it must be the will of the Lord.

One day when her husband, a civil engineer, was in a local dollar store, a salesgirl inquired about his wife's condition.

"She's in bed," he explained. "We have engaged a nurse."

"I have something here that helped me," said the girl. "Maybe it will help her."

She handed him a Unity publication. He stuffed it into his pocket. Sheepishly he gave it to his wife. "I don't propose that what the doctors haven't been able to do, reading something is going to do," he said.

His wife paged through the booklet, read portions of it, laid it aside. The next day she picked it up again. Her eyes lingered on the Prayer of Faith: God Is My Help in Every Need. . . .

She read it thoughtfully, put it away, read it again. The following day she memorized the stanzas and continued to repeat them slowly over and over in quiet affirmation, especially the lines which said,

> God is my health, I can't be sick,
> God is my strength, unfailing, quick;
> God is my all, I know no fear,
> Since God and Love and Truth are here.

A "feeling" came over her. Suddenly she realized she was moving her toes. Excitedly she summoned her husband and the nurse and insisted that she was healed. She was helped to her feet, and she took a few steps. When I visited her several weeks later she met me at the door and greeted me radiantly by saying, "I am healed."

There are spectacular and newsworthy healings in every faith, Christian and non-Christian alike, but as I stayed on at Unity Village and when, at night, I saw the lighted window of Silent Unity, I realized that it is here that the unacclaimed and unpublicized therapy of prayer goes on, moment by moment and day by day. It is here that the channel for Christ's healing is kept clear through denials and affirmations, through compassion and the remedy of truth.

The lighted window is the lighted heart, and Silent Unity is that light.

That is how Unity heals.

Its words and its voice go into lives the world around, believingly reminding them that: You Are God's Whole and Perfect Child. Every Cell in Your Body Is Aglow with His Light, Life, and Love.

CHAPTER EIGHT

Secrets of Unity's Success

It occurred to me during my Unity stay that there is an interesting contrast between those who train for the Unity ministry and the young men who take work in theological seminaries elsewhere in America.

One difference is in the student's approach to his vocation. There is nothing certain about a Unity minister's future, only that his faith is certain. There is no church waiting for him. He has no denominational status. No college placement bureau or pulpit committee or conference or bishop or superintendent is waiting to place him in just the right pulpit or pastoral appointment. The Unity graduate is an orphan, denominationally speaking, and he is well aware of this when he makes his decision to go into the Unity ministry.

In a way, this is one of the reasons for Unity's success. Every minister, man or woman, who has answered the Unity call has no illusion about the ministry being an easy road. Joyful it may be, and adventurous, but there is no guarantee of ease along the way. It is a hard-working job. Faith is a job. The morning lesson is a job. Opening a new frontier is a job. And so is building a center. But they are all jobs of joy.

There is the spirit of pioneering involved here and a fervor of spiritual conviction, qualities which, as I see the picture, are often lacking in the traditional church. *We* feel we have an established, going concern. Unity has no such illusions. We think in terms of material growth. Unity's ministers are indoctrinated with the growth of the spirit. We incline more and more to social status in our churches. Unity draws no such lines. There are Unity ministers, to be sure, who aspire to social standing and who will eventually become just as exclusive as many other ministers have become, but, generally speaking, Unity is a "classless" religion. And this is one of the reasons for Unity's success.

When I decided to study for the ministry in my parental faith, the German Reformed Church, I went from a sheltered home to a sheltered denominational college located in a sheltered rural area. (The church fathers had built the school there to keep the boys away from temptation.) I looked forward to a day, seven years later, when I would go out to serve a sheltered congregation.

While things have changed considerably in the years since then, many candidates for the Protestant ministry, no less than for the Catholic priesthood, still find a glaring gap between their life and the life of their parishioners. The problems confronting management and labor, the stresses and strains encountered by people in the workaday world, the triumphs and tragedies of both urban and rural people, most of whom look upon the church merely as another social phenomenon in American life, all are somewhat removed from parish premises as far as traditional religious leaders are concerned. There are exceptions, to be sure, but all too often the average ministerial student has been unable to identify himself with the experiences of the people he serves. There is, therefore, often a lack of confidence and an unbridged gap between pulpit and pew.

This problem is minimized in the case of Unity. By and large, the individual entering the Unity ministry has had some career experience or has already been successful in the business or professional field. Of the 182 men and women ordained by Unity during the past 10 years, 80% had had successful careers. Two had already retired from business even though they were relatively young men. Consequently, Unity worshipers recognize and feel a bond of understanding. Unity has never been a Sunday affair nor are its leaders known as a clergy class. One of Unity's secrets is that it moves among individuals as a visible and invisible fellowship *at the point where the worshiper lives.* Its leaders are quietly aware that people in the kind of system in which we live have problems that only God can, and does, solve, and that the minister must be able to help solve these problems.

Unity might never phrase it as I am phrasing it, but it seemed to me as I studied the Unity phenomenon "on location" here at Unity Village, that Unity tacitly recognizes that the individual in our modern culture is what I would call "pushed, pampered and poisoned." In all of these conditions Unity seeks to see the "Christ within the individual life," and not in any superior way, but as a matter of Christian course.

The individual in our culture, and in most cultures, is being pushed, pushed by schedules, by a sense of insecurity and need, by time, competition, money or the lust for money, and by fear. It should be a prerequisite for every religious leader to trade places periodically with the people to whom he ministers. He should know what it is like to move through city streets carrying a lunch box or to work the "graveyard shift." He should be able to put himself in the place of everyone in our competitive system to see what all too many clergymen have not seen: the pressure under which people live.

An investment broker confided to me that he spent thirty minutes in meditation every morning before going to his office. He lived in Beverly Hills and worked in downtown Los Angeles and by the time he had fought the freeway traffic, whipped the parking problem, and absorbed the

morning tension, his meditative reserve was all but used up!
On the other side of the continent, in New York, an adver-
tising agency employee once told me he did an hour of yoga
every morning. This, he claimed, sustained him with peace
and calm until noon! Then pressure began to build up.

To men of this type, to men of all types, Unity says, "Wait!
In the midst of activity, your mind can be tranquil. You are
ruled not by the world's mind, but by the Christ mind. God
is your help in every need. If you doubt it, you doubt God.
If you deny it, you deny God. You may think you are being
pushed, but you are actually being *pulled* by the love of the
Lord, pulled into peace and quietude of heart and mind."

And this kind of thinking, I have no doubt, is a reason for
Unity's success.

Modern man is also being pampered, and although Unity
might not state the proposition as I am stating it, it seems
to me that this pampering can have fatal consequences.
Never has there been a time when people have been made to
feel that they must be shielded and sheltered and spared the
shocks of life. Many a father has said to me, "I don't want
my son to go through what I had to go through in the depression. I don't want him to go through college the way I
had to, working in the cafeteria, janitoring in a dorm, mow-
ing the campus lawn." Recently when I asked a student in
one of my university classes why he had not brought his
notebook to class, he said, "I left it in my other car!"

All of this seemed more humorous to me as I thought of
it here at Unity, for somehow Unity Village gives a man a
contemplative view of things, and while you sense the seri-
ousness of life, you realize that nothing is quite *that* serious.
And you never doubt for a moment that man, through faith,
will come off victor in the long run.

Which is also one of Unity's secrets of success, for Unity
insists that man is in truth created in the image and likeness
of God and that his true self is the "Christ within."

But modern man *is* pampered. It is not only parents who pamper the children. Schools pamper the students. Churches pamper their congregations. The state pampers its people, and the nation pampers its citizens. It was truly a pampered world that I saw from my Unity vantage point! A world that could not build hospitals fast enough to take care of the pampered sick, or get enough psychiatrists to serve the pampered neurotics, or manufacture enough luxuries to adequately satisfy our luxury-pampered society.

The reason all this seemed so melodramatic or tragi-comic to me was because Charles Fillmore came to mind. If there was one thing Papa Charley opposed it was pampering himself. Even in his early nineties he was living as though he would never die. He married his second wife, Cora Dedrick, when he was seventy-nine. He went on speaking tours and wrote books when he was an octogenarian. Pampering, somehow, was not in the Fillmore vocabulary.

Lowell and Rick never knew the word, either. They always impressed me as men ready to outwork, outthink, and outdream most men half their ages. They seemed eager to demonstrate Unity's teaching that there is within us that inner strength, that inner reserve, that inner power, which is God. And that is why Unity says to this pampered age, "You are equipped to meet every situation. You are a radiating center of divine love. God in you can meet every need. Believe it. Know it. Recognize it!" These are tremendously necessary teachings for our shielded generation. Unity seeks to teach them and that is a reason for its success.

Viewing the life of our time from the standpoint of Unity, it became clear to me that people in the world were also in danger of being poisoned, poisoned by wrong thinking, by false impressions, by fear and apprehension about their future. I thought of a billboard which said, "One out of four will be a cancer victim. It could be you!" I remembered predictions which warned, "Four hundred Americans, will be killed over the holiday weekend." I recalled an ad that asked, "How often have you had to turn down a game of golf because there were checks and checks and more checks to be signed? Signing checks by hand is not the kind of exercise that keeps you in the pink. It is drudgery and dangerous to your health. Get a controlled signature machine." There came to mind a poster with a warning finger seeking me out as I drove by, a warning that screamed, "You may be the next mental patient!"

That is poison for the mind, and Unity knew it. It always knew that men are poisoned by drugs, by foods, and most of all by false beliefs, and it was doing something to combat it by way of denials and affirmations.

"Before I got into Unity," a man confessed to me, "I used to be against all religions except my own. I wanted to be friendly with them, but I thought God would not allow it." He, too, had been poisoned.

When he discovered Unity he learned that you cannot by any degree of logic or imagination ascribe to God a lower morality or sensitivity than you yourself possess. Unity offered him the antidote of a loving father who lived in him as his innate nature, and that, too, is a secret of the success of Unity.

When I asked Lowell Fillmore for his definition of innate or inner man, he said, "Innate is God's expression of man made in His own image and likeness, and because God is spirit, man, too, is spirit. Man's purpose in life is to realize himself as divine so that he may become a child of God in actuality."

To become this kind of a child of God, Unity believes and teaches that one should and can get rid of guilt. Guilt hangs over man like a mushroom cloud. We have been conditioned to guilt by an emphasis on inborn sin, and we are not quite sure that the taint of it has been washed away either by a mystical act of the church or by our faltering faith in Christ.

Most of us have been made to feel guilty when life is too good, for then we wonder whether it is right for us to enjoy such goodness in the midst of so much suffering in the world, and we have been made to feel guilty when life is burdensome because then something seems to tell us that this must be punishment for our awful transgression of God's law. We even have our guilt complexes in between, because by some strange quirk of conscience we seem to feel more secure in heaven's sight if we show signs of worry and concern. Spiritual schizophrenics, we find ourselves in a bad way! Unity, however, has a way out. It calls it the "Basic Principle" and it means a return to the truth that the life that Jesus Christ lived is the kind of life man basically has.

"Jesus," said Charles Fillmore, "represents God's idea of man in expression; Christ is that idea in the absolute. Jesus is Christ taking on the limitations of mortal consciousness, yet without sin; that is, not falling under the domination of evil thoughts." This means that every person becomes an individualized center of God-consciousess and implies that God's mind and God's power are ever available to each person through the realization of this truth.

There is, then, a tremendous personal quality about Unity. If the individual is one with God, then every person is also one with his fellow man. Then, too, humanity is an expression of creative force as is the universe, and all is in divine order.

This personal quality is an important factor in Unity's success. Religions that have grown old and large and institutionalized frequently lose the lustre of the personal touch, but Unity is young enough and small enough and sufficiently uninstitutionalized to still retain it. Consider, for instance, the letters that go out from *Silent Unity:*

Dear Friend: Our love infolds you! Our prayers infold the request you have made. Each such request is very near to our hearts, for we know that it is made in sincerity and with faith.

As we pray with you we are "knowing the truth." We are inclosing words of prayer that will help you to "know the truth," words that will establish you in faith, words that will enable you to pray effectively.

God's love infolds you. We are sure that you feel the presence and the power of this love and that you know that all is well.

Sincerely,
Silent Unity

Letters from Unity ministers are always highly personalized and spiritualized. No one writes better letters than Unity trained people. Unity gives you the feeling that you are important because God is important and because of this persuasion Unity has grown and will continue to grow just as long as it sincerely retains this quality.

Having assured the individual of his importance in God's scheme of things, Unity proceeds to make religion an exciting adventure. It does this largely by its metaphysical emphasis, pointing out that in metaphysics there is always a symbolical and mystical meaning penetrating beyond the obvious and factual into the hidden and the "real." Metaphysics is the cosmic dimension of physics, the understanding of the relationship between the material and the spiritual, between the world of change and appearance and the world of permanence and reality.

When Unity says, for example, "We believe in the twelve disciples," it means a good deal more than belief in twelve men called by Jesus as He walked by the lakeside.

"The twelve disciples," says Unity, "are symbolic of the twelve powers of man, going forth into mind and body to teach, preach, heal, and save man and the world from sin, sickness and death."

To explain this metaphysical content, Charles Fillmore prepared a diagram which correlated twelve nerve centers in man's body with twelve spirtual impulses. The center of the brain, he explained, corresponds to Faith and is exemplified by Peter; the loins, Strength, to Andrew; the pit of the stomach, Wisdom or Judgment to James the son of Zebedee; the back of the heart, Love, to John; the root of the tongue, Power, to Philip; the spot between the eyes, Imagination, to Bartholomew; the frontal brain, Will, to Matthew; the navel, Order, to James the son of Alphaeus; the medulla, Zeal, to Simon the Canaanite; the lower part of the back, Elimination, to Thaddeus; the generative function, Life, to Judas, and crowning this descriptive speculation is the aura of the "top brain" the "Great I Am" represented by Christ.

When this metaphysical interpretation of the simple fact that Jesus had twelve disciples first appeared just before the turn of the century, it was regarded as highly heretical and even downright silly by the traditional church. Some said it was a dreamed-up sensation to focus attention on a "new sect." Nothing could have been further from the truth.

Hermetic philosophy had already attuned the twelve powers to the twelve fundamental faculties of mind. It had also related these faculties to the twelve gates of the temple and to various other symbols which, like Ezekiel's vision, contain meanings within meanings, lessons within lessons, and circles of consciousness within circles of truth.

Fillmore was in good company and this fact is now beginning to be realized. He had drawn heavily upon the esoteric treasures of the past and today men are beginning once more to explore these treasures.

Ancient seers, long before the time of Christ, had already believed there are twelve "cosmic centers" in man and that by a mystical understanding of these an individual could learn to release the creative force localized in or channeled through them. Twelve had always been regarded as a sacred number. Kabbalists had their twelve uncompounded letters or characters which corresponded to twelve sensory and emotional impulses in man: sight, hearing, smell, speech, digestion, sexual intercourse, action, motion, wrath, mirth, meditation and sleep. Because God made everything by weight, number and measure, these also had their relationship to time and place. Then there were twelve signs of the zodiac, twelve sides to the Pythagorean symbol, twelve guides of man: two hands, two feet, two kidneys, the liver, the gall, the spleen, the colon, the bladder and the arteries. There were twelve tribes of Israel, twelve prophets, twelve stones on the breastplate of the Ephod, and many more recommendations that twelve consists of more than meets the eye!

All of which is evidence that Fillmore reached back into antiquity and confirmed the fact that there is a line of "apostolic succession" in the realm of metaphysics just as in the realm of ecclesiasticism. Today, with the interpenetration of outer space and the exploration of the inner man, with the quest for the invisible and the search for the unknown foremost in man's mind, Unity is metaphysically coming into its own. It seeks to open the uncut pages of the Bible and lead man into a new frontier of truth.

A major reason for Unity's success is at exactly this point: it presents the Bible as a living book, full of hidden meaning and unexplored paths. Up to now this best of best sellers is one of the least read of all best sellers. Pick up any hotel Bible and you will agree (Gideon statistics notwithstanding) that the copy is handsomely unused. Ask any Christian when he last dipped into the Scriptures and he will tell you it has been a long, long time. But when the Holy Book is read with metaphysics in mind, it comes to life.

Consider how Unity interprets a familiar incident such as the story of John the Baptist. "John the Baptist is an historical figure," says Unity, "but he is also a metaphysical truth representing the physical plane of existence, a voice in the wilderness, crying for the right way. When mortal mind strives to know and express more of the All-Possibility, when it realizes the shortcomings of the sense state, it cries out for a change. John the Baptist is a symbol of the struggle of the suppressed soul, the sin-sick, the hampered soul, in all who are weary of the material world and material ways. The remedy is 'Repent ye!' which means change your mind!"

It goes without saying that there are many Unity affiliates who believe that all one needs to do with metaphysics is to recognize these hidden forms. While this may prove efficacious, there is something deeper. There is the *living of the life* and it is at this point that Unity continues its persistent challenge for Christ-unfoldment. Not everyone is a healer just because he has memorized healing formulas, any more than a man is an artist because he is skilled in the fundamentals of art forms, or a chess expert because he has read books on chess. There must be something *within the man*.

Unity impressed itself upon me again during my Unity stay as consisting of truths that contain shallows in which a child can wade and depths in which a giant must swim. Unity represents a series of levels of truth and everyone is free to find his own.

The true metaphysician, like the true artist, must have the capacity for his art. This can never be anything contrived, and though it may certainly be developed, it is, first of all, an endowment. Everyone is artistic, but some are prodigies. Everyone is psychic, but some are sensitive. Everyone is religious by nature, but some are spiritual by endowment, and one of Unity's secrets is that it seeks out and develops this endowment in the individual according to the individual's capabilities.

Some critics have said that Unity made things too easy. They insisted that religion does not work on various levels. They said you cannot go from failure to success without a struggle and you cannot be brought from sickness to health by repeating denials and affirmations. A personality disorder, they made clear, is something deep-seated, and no one gets rid of it without the due process of some sort of theological conformity.

They overlooked one important point. The first step toward the new life is not faith in faith or belief in believability, but faith in an operative reality. This is what Unity is driving at. It inspires people to demonstrate what others may only declare. It urges an individual to live not as if God were true, but to live God as truth.

It is not really a new kind of faith, come to think of it, for Jesus said something about it long ago. A man running up to Him out of the multitude begged him to help his son who was possessed. "Master," he implored, "if thou canst do anything . . ." Jesus interrupted saying, "If you canst *believe* , . . all things are possible to him that believeth."

Then there is also the matter of Biblical literalism. Although Unity accepts the words of Jesus literally and metaphysically, it dares to raise questions which Christian laymen have wanted to ask for a long time and which, I dare say, have secretly annoyed clergymen in the institutionalized church. "How literally dare we interpret the Scriptures?" Or, to be more specific, "How valid, for example, are Paul's injunctions to the churches of *his* day for the churches of *our* day? Do his instructions to the congregations at Galatia, Ephesus, and Philippi apply to the churches, let us say, in Los Angeles, Cleveland, or Joliet, Illinois?"

Nearly 2000 years have passed into obscurity since Paul's ecclesiastical communiques were issued and none of his congregations remain. If they did, we would have appallingly little in common with them, especially when we remember that they lived under a form of "Christian communism" with a sense of values startlingly different than our own. Unity has dared to ask, "What shall we do about this? Shall we perpetuate beliefs out of which the meaning has gone?" And in asking these pointed questions, it has echoed the thoughts of many modern men both in and out of the church at large.

We are urged to be alert to world conditions; the early Christians were told to be insulated against the world. We are individualistic; but Paul's congregations were socialistic. We are commercially minded and consider money as an agent of good; they were non-commercial and looked upon money as an instrument of evil. Ours is a world of outer space; theirs was a world of the commune. Ours is the era of the hydrogen bomb; theirs was the era of the sword. Yet, for 2000 years Paul's opinions, theological, moral, and domestic have been accepted as "gospel" according to the early canonizers of Holy Writ.

Many a Christian has wondered about this and has wanted to make an issue of it, but it remained for Unity to come to grips with the subject. Without openly challenging any opinion or group, believing as it does that every man's quest contributes something to the total quest, Unity has, nonetheless, frankly asked, "How traditional must we be?"

When Paul advises Timothy that women should not teach or preach but should "learn in silence with subjection" does this apply to the women of today? When Paul admits to the Corinthians that, "I robbed other churches, taking wages of them to do you service," does this apply to modern Christendom as well and justify the principle involved? To be warned a thousand more years ago to stay away from those who have familiar spirits—does this rule out psychic research among contemporary Christians?

Unity takes texts literally only when they do not conflict with its concept of Truth, a process in which "inspired reason" plays a major part. Charles Fillmore was blunt enough to say that a man should exercise his common sense in reading the Bible as in reading anything else. In Unity, inspired reason and common sense are partners in the discovery of Truth, and not as a means for judging what should be accepted as *true* or ruled out as false.

That, too, is one of the secrets for Unity's growth.

There is a rare type of courage here, for any reading of Paul's letters or the Scriptures generally will persuade even the most fundamental literalist that churches today do not in fact subscribe to any view that is in serious conflict with the culture of our time, and certainly conform to no view that is in direct conflict with scientific proof. Yet there continues to be a great pretense among many groups that religion *should* abide by the letter of Biblical tradition.

Unity, without saying as much, has taken a long and quiet look at this duplicity and has soberly considered man's mania for perpetuating tradition for tradition's sake. It has also tacitly confirmed that it will have none of it. Religion is not a coat to be handed down from father to son uncritically or tried on for size uncomplainingly. It is a way of life.

The touchstone by which Unity evaluates the merit of spiritual teaching is at exactly this point, "How truthful is it in the light of our time and how truthful are we in our devotion to it?"

That is the basis of Unity training at Unity Village. "Learn nothing that is not truth, and teach nothing that is not true," is an academic principle here, and one reason for Unity's success is that this philosophy of teaching has found its way straight into Unity centers and into the hearts of the people.

Charles Fillmore once said, "It is not safe to assert positively that a single paragraph of the Bible is understood in our day as it was intended at the time it was written. It is the spirit, rather than the letter of the text, that those worship who have within them the true Christ principle."

"What have you found in Unity?" I asked people at Unity Village and at Unity centers in cities and towns. "What have you found in Unity?" They said:

> An honesty about religion.
> A teaching that makes sense.
> Physical healing.

The inspiration of *Daily Word*.
A challenge.
A religion that can be lived.
Practical teachings.
A wonderful Sunday School for my children.
A new approach to religion.
No talk about sin or punishment.
A happy religion.
A God of love.
Creative power of thoughts and words.
Prosperity.
The meaning of prayer.
Not to be afraid of God.
The real meaning of Jesus Christ.

They may not have known it, they may never have admitted it, but they discovered all these things because they came seeking. They came in the spirit of the quest and learned that to dwell upon goodness is to become the recipient of all that is good. To be joyful is to attract more joyfulness. To meditate on love is to grow lovely in the inner self. To think health is to be healthy. To put your life into God's love is to put God's love into your life.

It is a profound Unity secret which says: you can change your consciousness. And that is what happens to people in Unity. Their thinking changes. Their approach to life changes. Their divine nature begins to ascend. Their "Christ mind" starts to function. The "God within" is permitted to take over and a new being has been born!

I once heard Emmet Fox in Carnegie Hall. Influenced by Unity, trained in truth, author of the ever-popular *The Sermon on the Mount*, Emmet Fox referred to himself as one of Charlie Fillmore's spiritual children and said,

Do not try to think out in advance what the solution of your difficulty will turn out to be. Do not outline in advance. Leave the question of ways and means strictly to God. You want to get out of your difficulty, that is sufficient. You do your half, God will never fail to do His . . .

Everything in your life today, the state of your body, whether healthy or sick, the state of your fortune, whether prosperous or impoverished, the state of your home, whether happy or unhappy, the present condition of every phase of your life is entirely conditioned by the thoughts and feelings which you have entertained in the past, by the habitual tone of your past thinking.

The condition of your life tomorrow, and next week and next year, will be entirely conditioned by the thoughts and feelings which you choose to entertain from now on. In other words, as you choose your thoughts, so you choose your life. You cannot have one kind of mind and another kind of environment.

Unity's secret can best be understood in such terms. Truth is primarily concerned with spirit and spirit embraces man's total relationship to God and orientation in the kind of world that God has made. It may be difficult for some men to understand, but it is true nonetheless that a right view of God is more needful than riches, and a knowledge of truth is better than bread. It is, in fact, this kind of spiritual bread that Unity dispenses.

For a little while here at Unity Village I felt the reality of Unity's secrets, though I also realized I had only partially comprehended the boundaries of the kingdom of heaven which man is here invited to seek. Yet, to demand anything else; money, food, or material well-being, before claiming the "kingdom" is, according to Unity, putting the cart before the horse.

I heard a Unity member say, "My desire for God is always so much greater than my needs, that my needs are automatically dissolved in my desiring." She meant this literally, having reached a point where her search for truth ruled out any anxiety for the morrow.

Others had already told me how they used to strive and toil for things, only to find that things eluded them. Then, turning their efforts and their loyalties to the discernment of truth, the things they had sought followed as a natural consequence.

I would be the last to say that life does not work this way for everyone who has the will to believe it, the faith to live it, and the confidence to expect it. Something *does* happen when a believer seeks the kingdom for the kingdom's sake. Unexpected blessings *are* showered upon him and mysterious doors *are* opened for his good.

What was it Charles Fillmore said? "God is, and we are. Let us live in His world—not a world to be tomorrow, next month, next year, or next century, but *here and now*. God's beautiful universe is all about us, only awaiting our acknowledgment of its presence. Let us know God and live, live with love and joy, health and peace, here evermore."

It could well be that Unity's secret of success is actually as simple as that.

CHAPTER NINE

What Unity Believes
About Life After Death

In Unity, strangers simply do not exist.

This is particularly true at Unity Village as I realized on Friday night when I sat with a group of some twenty students and visitors in the motel lounge. We were talking about life after death and as far as the interest and exchange of ideas were concerned, we might all have conceivably been friends of long standing. It might even have been that in some previous existence we had gone through all this before, sitting together as a group and discussing the uncatchable mystery of what happens in the great beyond.

Even while we talked animatedly about this fascinating subject, I remembered the words of Lowell Fillmore who once said to me, "Unity's emphasis is on life *here* rather than in the hereafter. We feel that if we can make this life the very best life we possibly can, the hereafter will take care of itself. Unity is partly a turn-away from religions that put the main emphasis on preparation for death. Unity says, 'Live! Live now! Live fully!'"

Lowell was unquestionably right. Unity, like the well-known opinion of Oscar Wilde, was saying, "One world at a time, please!" Nonetheless, on this Friday night we were cutting the pages of the sealed book, as seekers have done since time began.

I told the group that one of my instructors in creative writing once said, "Never write about anything morbid, like death or dying. In the first place nobody knows anything about it excepting those who have experienced it and they won't tell, and, secondly, nobody wants to read about dying because they don't believe it will happen to them anyway."

We agreed that a great change had taken place in our thinking since the outspoken professor laid down this dictum. People *are* interested in what happens after death, and, furthermore, the subject need not be morbid. If we go to a strange country, should we not find out about it before we go and learn a bit about its life and customs? People have more questions about life's continuum than they ever had, part of which may be due to the precariousness of the world in which we live and the feeling that one false military move could joust us into that other world in less time than it takes to tell.

I mentioned that wherever I went in my lecture work, whether to college campuses or religious conferences, the topic of life after death was always high on the agenda, and on this Friday night at Unity Village I recognized that men and women of Unity have some answers which would be helpful to other groups.

My investigation of so-called mediums came into the discussion, and I told my listeners that these experiences included the meaningful and the meaningless, the genuine and the faked, the evidential and the questionable, all of which are part of the vast arc of research in this intriguing field.

As we talked about these things in front of the open fireplace—fireless on this balmy Friday night—and helped ourselves to coffee and doughnuts and fruit of various kinds, it was always easy to come back to the words, "Live now! Live fully!" At the moment, part of this good living consisted of friendly discussion.

I was assured that Charles Fillmore had been interested in spiritualism at an early stage in his life, but that he dropped it abruptly and warned against it. He felt that there were some valid psychic phenomena, but he wondered about the merit of it all and the demerit of it. The demerit lay in the fact that many persons went overboard on spiritualism, began to depend on discarnate spirit guidance, and looked to mediums for help more than they looked to God.

Papa Charley figured, and rightly, that since the dead apparently knew little more about life than did the living, what was the good of all this mediumistic clairvoyance, clairaudience, and attempts at materialization? If messages, when they did come through, consisted merely of trivia, why waste time on them? And why seek to prove that death does not end all when Jesus Christ had conclusively proved that already?

Furthermore, Fillmore contended, since we have access to the spirit of Jesus Christ and to the Christ mind, why not spend the time in making this contact? This persuaded him to warn Truth seekers that they stay away from spiritualism. "We teach spiritual Truth," he proclaimed, "and Truth and spiritualism are as wide apart as the poles."

But his major contribution to Unity's belief in this whole field was that God did not create man to die. I was eager to discuss this point with the group, but they settled back and wanted me to define the position of the institutionalized church in the field of life after death. This was fair enough, but I had to submit that Christian opinions about immortality vary all the way from belief in an instantaneous, miraculous transportation of the soul to God's throne, to the theory that the dead remain somberly in their graves until some specially appointed resurrection morn. The average Protestant would be hard put to articulate his deepest convictions about the world beyond.

Hell is definitely "out" as far as liberal Protestantism is concerned, and heaven is being re-examined, just as the Catholic is re-appraising purgatory, and as the fundamentalist is re-evaluating in the light of science, many of the notions he once irrevocably held about the Promised Land.

Surely, I had to say, heaven and hell are now spiritually interpreted by the church at large as conditions in consciousness and not as geographic locations. Heaven and hell are areas of awareness in which the soul or psyche or spirit continues its development nearer to the reality of God than was possible on this four-dimensional physical plane. Golden streets, heavenly thrones, harps and halos, no less than alabaster stairs and wings for flying are fantasies of the past. The "many mansions" are no longer etheric apartment dwellings, but, according to modern theology, states of mind or of being. This, it occurred to me, all came startlingly close to Unity's original idea when, in one of his bold declarations, Charles Fillmore said, "We believe all the doctrines of Christianity *spiritually interpreted!*"

"What about final judgment?" one of the young men wanted to know, saying that he and a fundamentalist had been discussing that the other day.

I submitted that the institutionalized church, generally, still insisted on a divine reckoning of some kind, but the nature of this judgment was also being rethought in ecclesiastical circles. Degrees of punishment and rewards were still basic in the church's thinking, but there was a good deal of uncertainty about how delicate the scale was attuned on which man's virtues and vices would be weighed. Persisting in the Christian's thinking was the redemptive work of Christ, but there were those who believed with Unity that, "through conscious union with Jesus in the regeneration, man can transform his body and make it perpetually healthy, therefore immortal, and that in this way man can attain eternal life."

Beyond this, what did Unity believe about life after death? And what about the intriguing supposition that God did not intend that man should die?

It was Friday night, an appropriate time to discuss these things, and in this friendly room I was soon able to synthesize what Unity generally believed and what Unity headquarters proclaimed.

First of all, Unity believes in reincarnation, but in a way that must be rather carefully explained. What, after all, is reincarnation? It is the belief that the essence of man, his life force, returns to express itself after death in another time, in another place, and in another body, until it finally gains divine perfection and lives eternally—for God never intended that man should die.

I reminded the group of something they already knew far better than I, namely, that Charles Fillmore, with blunt courage, once declared, "The western world in general looks upon reincarnation as a heathen doctrine. Many persons close the door of their mind upon it without waiting to find out what message it brings when interpreted in the light of truth."

Then he interpreted it. He saw reincarnation as a process leading toward eternal life in a manner not unlike that proposed by the great religions of the East. In all of these religions is the hint that man must be born again and again because he has not yet learned how to *live*. When he learns how to live, he will cease learning how to die. In other words, when man learns how to live to his utmost spiritual capacity, he will live forever, and reincarnation will have served its purpose. It is a temporary measure only.

That is what Charles Fillmore affirmed and, when he was accused of being a bit of a heathen in his own thinking, he replied, "Through the light of the indwelling Christ the so-called heathen have discerned many truths to which the more material-minded people of the newer countries have been blind. Whenever there has been a nation of thinkers who were not bound in materialism, those thinkers have accepted reincarnation as a fact. It is rejected only where the craze for wealth and for fame and for the things of the world has darkened the mind with materiality."

With this in mind, I asked the group, "But how do you think reincarnation works?"

"It is like putting a new light bulb in place of one that has burned out," a student suggested. "The power of God is the circuit."

"Death is actually a process of birth," said another.

"Reincarnation is simply part of the total life cycle," said a third.

Differences, however, between Unity's belief in reincarnation and Hindu and Buddhist beliefs were thoroughly aired in our evening rendezvous. For one thing—and quite obviously—Unity never believed, as some Hindu sects do, in transmigration of souls, by which is meant the retrogression of spirits into a lower state of existence. Nor was reincarnation interpreted in a strictly Eastern sense. To Eastern, non-Christian groups, reincarnation is an evolutionary process, a chain of cause and effect. To Unity, it is a "unifying force" through which God seeks to restore man to his original deathless state.

In this connection, interestingly enough, Unity believes that death came into the world through the Adamic man and this resulted in body dissolution. But in the demonstration of the overcoming of death, as shown in the resurrection of Jesus Christ, the restoration of the "lost Eden" is already begun.

To the Hindu and Buddhist, reincarnation is inseparable from the law of karma, which is the ethical consequence of the process of cause and effect. The Hindu carries with him the result of his previous acts and is tied, in a very real sense, to karmic law. His life is the net result of his conduct in a previous existence. Fillmore referred to the Hindu as "a weary treadmill traveler from birth to death and from death to birth." I suggested that Hindus and Buddhists would not agree with this interpretation, but Fillmore, even as Albert Schweitzer, saw Hinduism as a philosophy of life-negation and Christianity as a process of life-affirmation.

Fillmore contended that the regenerative work of Christ released man from the karmic wheel and prepared him for new life, a series of new lives, in fact, which might be looked upon as vehicles for the attainment of the perfect, deathless body *which spirit already embodies within itself in every phase of life.* That is to say, man already includes within himself all that he is one day to become.

"Through repeated trials at living, man is discovering that he must learn to control the issues of life," Fillmore insisted. "The divine law, as taught by Jesus, must be understood and applied to all life's details, and when this is done, the 'Eden state' will be restored and man will live forever."

A member of the group had an interesting observation. "Is it possible," he wondered, "that Charles Fillmore might have been thinking also in terms of life expectancy and could he perhaps have been quite right in his assumption that if man does learn how to live properly, man may live forever? After all, life expectancy has been steadily rising. A child born these days may expect to live until he is seventy. In Papa Charley's day, the life expectancy was only fifty. If each generation can add ten or fifteen years to the span of life, given time, we will be living awfully long! If we add spiritual know-how to physical know-how, inasmuch as the body is, after all, a single unit, it might well be possible to reach a state where man need never die."

Another participant in our discussion had an equally interesting theory. He proposed that because Eastern people did not have our creature comforts and conveniences, they did not have our "will to live" and consequently occupied themselves more with thoughts of dying. We, enjoying our way of life, are more inclined to think in terms of living! Dying, he proposed, is more unpopular in the Western world than it is in the East.

Be that as it may, I discovered that death is looked upon by Unity as the great negation which will one day be overcome. It is a circumstance which should neither be feared nor welcomed. It is a kind of neutral state, progressive only as man learns that it can eventually lead him to a full knowledge of his spiritual union with God. The key-thought in Unity remains: God did not intend that man should die. But because of the present *fact* of death, Unity accepts it as it does many other facts, the fact of sickness, for example, or poverty or darkness. They are facts, not truths, and each will be vanquished in its turn: sickness by the truth of health, poverty by the truth of substance, darkness by the truth of light, and finally death by the truth of life.

Unity accepts death impartially, as a man might accept the act of going to sleep. This was underlined by a reminder of the popular Indian expression, "Why should I fear to die? I die every night!"

We concluded that death is a rest period, preparing man for his awakening to another day of adventure. Death is that part of life that prepares a person for more and greater living. Death is an error of mind, the great negation which must itself be negated.

There is no room in the Unity eschatological system for a heaven filled with busybody souls living a "spiritually suburban" kind of life. Fillmore contended that mortal mind created such an idea of heaven in the first place, a heaven where "all the old family relationships are as man knows them in his present life." Personal consciousness is insufficient to demonstrate eternal life," said Fillmore. "The great family of Christ, the whole redeemed Adam race is all *one,* and the little selfish relationships of the Adam man have no place in the new order."

All of which may have been another reason why Lowell Fillmore insisted that all men should, "Live now! Live fully!" Heaven, true heaven, can only be a kingdom in which *all* men have learned how to live. Heaven must of necessity be incomplete unless *all* men have finally become overcomers of death. It is logically true that in any real heaven, spiritual kinship will be more important than family relationships, and in heaven the consciousness of all mankind will need to approximate the consciousness of God.

While such conclusions seemed to me comparable to the Nirvanic state described in Hinduism and Buddhism, my listeners would not carry the analogy that far. Unity's main basis of agreement with Eastern religions lay in the fact that reincarnation provides the most equitable plan for the total understanding of life.

Surely a just and righteous God would see to it that every soul has repeated and equal opportunities to work out his salvation. A deformed child, a premature death, a sudden tragedy, all of these, no less than the young genius, the gifted prodigy, the talented mind—each has a meaning and each is an argument for reincarnation.

"A single span of life," Fillmore insisted, "does not constitute man's entire opportunity for life."

We concluded that more and more people are beginning to agree with this point of view, that more and more interest is being shown in reincarnation, and that more and more persons are being drawn to Unity where they can freely discuss these issues without being criticized or accounted queer.

I submitted to the group that my files are full of letters from people who feel they have had psychical experiences and who are reluctant to discuss such phenomena with their minister. They tell me that they would simply be told that "such impressions are the work of the devil," or that they are imagining things, or that they had better see a psychiatrist. Unity is different. Although it does not endorse psychism and although every Unity leader is acquainted with Charles Fillmore's stand on the matter, Unity is ready to deal understandingly with those who have questions in this field.

Judging from this Friday night seminar, most Unity students would preface any psychical investigation with Lowell Fillmore's tactical injunction, "Live! Live now! Live fully!" And they would agree with him that, "Unity is more interested in life here than in the hereafter." Which reminded me that in my research among the many religions of the world, few brought the spirit of living so fully into the whole spectrum of life as Unity does.

You realize this at a Unity memorial service. It is a simple service devoid of morbidity and shorn of doleful hymns or funereal eulogies. Here are none of the "ashes to ashes, dust to dust" references, or reminders of the well-worn phrase, "when worms destroy this body"; no macabre viewing of the body of the departed. Here, where cremation is the rule, the service is one of emphasis upon the beauty and serenity of life, together with God's good in the living of it.

As to grief and mourning, these, too, are brought into a new perspective. After our meeting, one of the Unity men referred me to an article by William A. Clough in which, with typical Unity approach, the persuasive thesis is proclaimed that:

"Grief is not a sign of weakness, for the greatest men have known deep grief. But they have manifested their greatness by rising above and overcoming their grief by claiming the joy that is their rightful heritage. Grief is human; joy is divine.

"Grief is part of human nature, but joy is part of our divine nature. . . . Prolonged mourning may be an indication of too great self-concern. We are mourning then not for the one who has gone, but for ourselves. When the letter 'u' is taken from the word *mourning*, the word becomes *morning*, the dawn of a new day!"

Contrasting this point of view with the customary reflection on death, I realized that Unity as a religion is not interested in conforming to ancient presuppositions, but is eager to explore new approaches to one's attitude toward both life and death. I suppose a person can better show his love for someone by adjusting to life than by bemoaning death, and I thought again that there is probably no better way of demonstrating one's faith than by the constant reminder that though death is truly a fact, it is *not* a fact in Truth.

After our good-nights were said, I went for a walk in the Unity grounds, asking myself how often men and women had speculated on immortality in closed rooms, only to find their assurance of it under the starlit sky. I found such assurance as I walked alone. I sensed it in the night sounds, felt it in the hush of Unity Village, and was reminded of it whenever I saw the lighted Tower.

Surely there is an unbroken line of questing souls in all faiths all around the world who keep the hope of immortality alive by their knowledge that God is life, that all is life, and life is God. But this, I realized anew, requires faith, and faith requires reflection.

Men and women of the Unity persuasion find this faith in the quest, in the process of search and discovery. They also find it as they reflect upon their founders who gave them examples in how to live and how to deal with death. Charles and Myrtle Fillmore approached their passing like adventurers preparing for a rendezvous with life, hearing clairaudiently, I dare say, the opening door, feeling intuitively the pulse of the divine, seeing anew the visions that had guided them throughout their years. It is well known that at the passing of Charles Fillmore, he looked up and said, "Do you see it? The new Jerusalem, coming down from God, the new heaven and the new earth! Don't you see it?"

And I wondered how often he walked these grounds at night, thinking the thoughts we had been thinking, asking the questions we had asked, and speculating, as we had in our discussion, how it all fit into the puzzle of life.

I understood Charles Fillmore better just now than ever before. I understood what he meant when he said that perhaps he would never die. He may have meant this quite literally, having foreseen for himself what some modern scientists are now predicting for men of the future: a scientific breakthrough which, together with our ever-increasing knowledge about the nature of life, will make the saying a reality: God did not intend that man should ever die.

As the stars looked down over Unity Village it occurred to me that Charles Fillmore may very well have been right in his theory but wrong in his calculation. *Some day* it will happen. Through someone, somewhere, the truth will be demonstrated. And who is to say who that someone is or who he was?

Right in theory, but wrong in calculation. Is this not often true of men who, by a destiny beyond our knowing, live ahead of their time?

CHAPTER TEN

Unity: An Appraisal

It was Saturday morning and my Unity week was rapidly drawing to a close. The afternoon would find me back on the highway returning to my post at the university and as I walked to the cafeteria the sound of traffic was already more distinct than it had been during the past few days.

After breakfast I returned to my motel with the avowed purpose of doing some much needed writing. My typewriter was set up, the yellow sheets were handily in place, and I was just getting set for some good hours of work when there was a rap at the door.

What could I do but say to myself, "No one cometh unto me excepting the Father hath sent him!"

The visitor was an acquaintance of long standing who considered it a pleasant surprise that he had found me. A relaxed, portly, middle-aged man, he was public relations counselor for a nationally-known industry. He had been in New Orleans with his wife where they had met her sister, a Unity member. She was riding to Chicago with them and, since none of them had ever been to Unity Village, they decided to take this route and look things over. Paging through the guest register at the Tower and spying my name, he decided to begin the tour with a stop at Motel unit #1.

It occurred to me that perhaps the Father *had* sent him, and not him only, but his wife and her sister as well, for a more interesting or diversified trio would have been hard to find. An ardent Protestant layman, the man of the party had met me at religious conferences at Green Lake in Wisconsin and once at a Chicago meeting. He was, to quote his favorite phrase, "on a quest, just like you."

His wife, an outward-going, pleasantly irrepressible woman, flashing diamonds and wrapped in a mink stole knew emphatically what she believed and why she believed it. I had met her previously and she was delighted that I remembered that she was an Episcopalian "not by birth, but by choice and intellectual persuasion," as she once put it. Her sister, a widow, a charming, gray-haired woman with a spontaneous smile, was already strolling somewhat enraptured along the walk breathing deeply of the bracing Unity air. There was no question that she had found a faith and that this was it.

This was the end of my good intentions for a writing spree and when my friend suggested as an aside that perhaps they were disrupting my day, I caught myself saying, "Not at all. I am sure everything is in divine order!"

I rather think it was, and I assured them that if they wanted to see Unity Village I would be their guide until they found someone better. In taking them over the course, I would be familiarizing myself with it once more, and even though the workers had their Saturday off, Rick and Lowell and others of the staff would very likely be on hand.

But most of all it was "in divine order" to realize that the world had come to Unity in these three visitors, for here I had a "convert," a "seeker," and an "observer" solid in her faith. And I? Well, I was the momentary appraiser.

Because the convert wanted to walk through the grounds on her own to "get the feeling of Unity Village," the seeker, the observer, and I strolled over to the amphitheatre where we sat for a moment in the quiet of the pleasant surroundings.

"How do you account for it?" the observer, my friend's wife, wanted to know.

"Account for what?" her husband, the seeker, asked.

"Why, all of this," she said with a flourish that took in not only the amphitheatre but the Normandy homes peeping through the trees. "I had no idea when Bertha talked about Unity that it was so pretentious. How old is it? Fifty, sixty years? How do you account for it?"

"Why," exclaimed the seeker, "you account for it on the basis that people want it and need it."

"Oh, but darling," she replied, "there are goodness knows how many religions in the world."

"There are goodness knows how many cars, too," he countered, biting off the end of a cigar.

"But why another religion? Why Unity?" she insisted.

I thought she was asking me, but the husband was answering because he thought it preposterous that a religion had to account for itself any more than a new automobile had to justify its appearance. If someone felt he had a better religion or a better car, let him put it on the market. Let the people decide.

I sat there thinking that Unity could be accounted for in quite another way. It justified itself by being one religious movement which came to create a fellowship where people are held together by the adventure of the quest and the thrill of discovery. It justified itself by seeking individuals who would be held together without knowing exactly what it is that holds them—unless it be the spirit of Truth.

"I account for Unity," I had to say, "on the basis that it gives us a view of what the world can be and on the basis that the essential activity of an individual is his spiritual consciousness."

"But don't all religions believe that?" asked the observer.

"I am sure they do," I said, "and that is what accounts for *them.*"

"By the way," the seeker spoke up with cigar and lighter in hand, "it is all right to smoke here, isn't it?"

I assured him it was.

"Unity members smoke, I'm sure they do," said his wife confidently. "And they drink, too. I'm sure they do. Don't they?" she asked.

"I think we'd have to say that moral codes among Unity members vary with individuals."

"Bertha says they are all vegetarians," mused the observer.

"In principle, perhaps," I corrected. "Rarely in practice. Although basically, Charles Fillmore strongly opposed meat eating."

"Well, now, there you are," concluded the observer. "That is the way these new religions get started. They stress some particular phase of life and that attracts people. Now you take Bertha. When Tim, that was her husband, when Tim died she said that Unity sustained her as no other religion could possibly have done. How does she know? How could she say that? *My* religion sustained me when our son was killed in Japan."

"We are all different, Emily," said the husband consolingly. "One finds his answer here, another there. But a religion like Unity has a wide range of speculation. Bertha goes for that. I sort of go for that—as you do," indicating me with the glowing tip of his cigar. "I think there is more to life and death than most churches admit. More to religion generally, for that matter. A religion like Unity explores all these roads."

"What roads?" Emily wanted to know.

"Oh, like reincarnation," he submitted. "The way God works. The way prayer works. The way positive thinking and the power of the mind work. You see, Unity has all these sayings and things, these affirmations and the like, and I think that's good. It opens up a whole new field of operation."

"It is an interesting point," I agreed. "By the use of techniques we get to know ourselves and our potential. As we get to know ourselves we get to know God, and getting to know God helps us to know our fellowman. Unity is an experimental faith and that means that people are working at it."

"You think that is good?" asked the observer as if she felt it might be a bit of presumptive evidence about any religion to say that it is experimental.

"I believe it is good," I had to say. "A Christian, or the devotee of any religion, should by rights be involved in an experiment with the supranormal. Religion is belief in supernatural revelation. As I see it, Unity operates in a supernatural world even though it continually tells us that miracles are really not miracles, but simply the operation of divine law. Nonetheless, Unity is deeply involved in experiences above the common norm. Unity people depend upon the supernatural no matter what they call it. They depend upon it, trust in it, and base their hope on it. In everything a true Unity follower sees and experiences, he finds a touch of God, not always understandable, mind you, and not always directable according to his wish, but it is there. The ways of the world are not his ways. The solutions to problems always take God into account. A Unity follower is the kind who gets up in the morning to greet the day as though it were a new gift from God, and who does not consider it odd or queer to be continually thankful for the fact of living."

"Well, that's Bertha!" the observer agreed.

"And I don't see anything wrong about it," said the seeker.

"Who said there was anything wrong?" Emily asked. "All I am saying is that all religions have these things."

How far could I go without appearing to be a spokesman for Unity? I decided to let Bertha tell them sometime, if she wished, how far this adventurous spirit was carried forward in Unity. For my part, I secretly believed it was one quality that actually kept Unity young and Unity followers young, too. It was the adventurous quest that kept them spiritually on their toes, and lured them all. For them, as I once said, life was a drama and the playwright was God, and they were helping Him in the preparation of the script.

The letter that came just when you were wondering when the person would write, the friend who showed up unannounced exactly when needed, the job that was offered when all seemed hopeless, the check that arrived in the nick of time, all were meaningful, all were part of life's adventure with the supernormal, and all were part and parcel of the Unity point of view.

Which prompted me to say that I thought one of Unity's distinctives was its light touch, or, as Unity ministers might say, "its touch of light."

I tried to explain it by saying, "Unity, by looking at the bright side of life, is continually turning things around. It sees life in terms of hypothetical cases, cases that always permit a choice, and urges a man to choose the better of the two, the higher rather than the lower, the hopeful rather than the hopeless, the greater rather than the smaller, the lovelier rather than the loveless, the God of light rather than the god of darkness."

We found ourselves in agreement that such an enunciation of the power of choice changes life. It turns things around or else it turns the individual around so that his world becomes a new and different world. Yet all of this is within the framework of the world *as it is*. The world of men with all its problems, suffering, and sorrow exists, but it is literally being towed toward betterment by the light touch or the touch of light. Progress must always be from the basis of goodness and not from the basis of evil.

Convinced that this is true, persuaded that God is good and that His love and truth are expressed through you, persuaded that every circumstance is full of meaning, life takes on an observational quality which adds to the adventure. You can now stand back and look at yourself, getting a perspective on how God is using you in His scheme of things. Part of the Unity viewpoint involves the secret of getting yourself off your hands, of losing yourself in the discovery of your particular mission in life, and of placing yourself at the disposal of divine guidance.

To all of this the seeker agreed and the observer murmured that I was probably taken in by Unity more than I realized.

"Don't you find anything in Unity to criticize?" she said with a laugh.

"Of course he doesn't," said her husband. "Unity has taught him to see only the good."

"I always find things to criticize," I confessed, "even in my own religion."

"Which reminds me," the observer cut in shaking a finger at me, "just what *is* your religion?"

"Denominationally?" I asked.

"Denominationally," she said.

"It is a bit involved," I answered, "but let's say that I still belong to the church of my birth."

"Which is?"

"The German Reformed," I explained, "which merged with the Evangelical Synod of North America which later merged with the Congregational Church which had merged with the Christian Church and which formed the United Church of Christ which may soon be merging with the Methodist Church and the United Presbyterian Church and, incidentally, with your Episcopal Church!"

"Then," she declared getting up and clasping my hand, "you will be in most excellent company!"

With this we walked from the amphitheatre, following the graveled roadway in the direction of the quadrangle. As we made our way past the Inn to the Silent Unity building, the seeker said, "I would like to follow up Emily's question, if you don't mind. What do you find to criticize in Unity?"

"I think the greatest criticism of Unity is the criticism I would have of any church and of my own religious orientation," I said. "I mean the closing of the gap between profession and practice. Any faith that can accomplish this will be the most vital faith in all the world and will be the religion which the world of tomorrow—and today—will follow and take seriously. When Unity members get just as upset with the world as does anyone else, when they widen the gap between prayer declared and prayer demonstrated, when they cease having distinctives so that anyone associating with them fails to find something special in the way of techniques, when they lose their deep relationship with the supernatural, then Unity has lost its meaning."

"Is Unity losing it?" asked the seeker.

"No, I don't think so. But every so-called convert and surely every oncoming Unity generation must live the life anew and be re-dedicated to it. There is no guarantee that any religion is here to stay. I wonder, too, whether Unity realizes the challenge confronting it and whether it has the will to explore new frontiers, because, you see, the churches are catching up and, if not the churches, then at least individuals are, and they need continually new and inspired leadership."

"That is exactly what I said to my sister on the way up here," said Emily. "She talked about Unity's emphasis on spiritual healing. Well, now, we have a very important program of spiritual healing in the Episcopal church and everybody knows it."

"Most churches nowadays stress healing," said her husband, "but I think they may have been badgered into it by these newcomers like Unity and Christian Science and others."

"There is a very good point here," I agreed. "I believe

Charles Fillmore was one of the foremost leaders in the field of positive thinking. But today many ministers in the traditional churches are becoming highly skilled in spiritual therapy. They have set up prayer groups, experimental clinics, and have impressive records in this field. This was not true in the early days of Unity. Fifty years ago spiritual healers and metaphysicians stood outside the pale of the church. Of course, Unity will say that it does not matter how or where spiritual healing finds its way into people's lives. And, furthermore, healing is just *one* of Unity's contributions in the spiritual field."

But as I said this we had reached the main Unity grounds and now we stood beneath the lighted window. As I explained what I knew about Silent Unity, I wondered whether healing was not now and would not always remain man's greatest need and Unity's greatest contribution to religion. Because I admired Unity as a total spiritual movement, I wanted to say, "May that light never dim and may that dedication never cease, and may there always be workers in the world who send forth that light. Healing is not only of the body. It is of the mind and the heart and the spirit and the whole consciousness of man and all mankind. Let there be healing and there need never be any question as to whether or not there will be happiness and hope and peace and good will on earth."

"So this is the place of Silent Unity," the seeker said with feeling, and what I will remember most about his saying that was that he instinctively looked around for a place where he could dispose of his cigar! To the annoyance of his wife, he finally tamped it down in the rose garden. "I have heard some remarkable things about Silent Unity," he was saying. "Have you checked on any of their results?"

"I have," I said.

"You believe they're genuine?"

"I do," I said, "especially where you get a circuit of faith among all parties concerned; the patient, and those related in any way to the patient, Silent Unity and all those related in any way to Silent Unity. With such a combination, with people believing not only that God is on their side, but that they are on God's side, I would be the last to limit the so-called miraculous."

"They use all sorts of methods, don't they?" my friend asked. "Prayer, suggestion, all of that?"

"Yes, I don't think you would offend Unity by saying it uses the power of suggestion or the power of any other therapy. One Unity minister once told me, 'We use any tool that works. If the proper suggestion can effect the proper cure, that may be God's way of working.' "

"There is one thing I don't understand," said the observer. "Bertha tells me they do not use the sacraments. Our church uses them in its healing program."

"That is certainly true," I admitted. "And I think many people coming to Unity might miss the use of such sacraments as the Lord's Supper or Baptism or Extreme Unction. Here these are not observed. Here we find an almost Quaker-like simplicity and a strictly metaphysical interpretation of these traditional observances. Baptism in Unity is actually a type of blessing and the belief in the anointing by the Holy Spirit. As to Communion, this, too, is interpreted symbolically. The blood of Jesus represents eternal life, and the broken bread symbolizes incorruptible substance. Neither would Extreme Unction be found in Unity. It would be, instead, a kind of spiritual unction, the result of prayer and affection bestowed upon the dying."

"Well," said the seeker, "there are things a man simply believes and he doesn't ask for any justification for the belief. What is a sacrament after all but a symbol for something else that is taking place? I always feel as you do," he said to me, "that if religious leaders would be willing to sit down together and discuss the deepest meaning of their beliefs they would find they are much closer to agreement than they ever realized."

"Yes, but darling," said Emily, "they can't *all* be right."

"Probably not," he replied, "and they can't all be wrong."

"I agree with you," I had to admit to my friend, the seeker. "That a man believes what he wills to believe is an old theory of mine, and it has been strengthened during my week here at Unity. There *are* things a man simply believes, believes uncritically but so deeply that the wisest theologians with all their skills, and the hardest-crusted realists with all their proofs, cannot shake that man's belief. Something has happened to him inside. He not only believes, he knows, and he not only knows, he has experienced his knowing. You will never argue such a man either in or out of a religion."

At this moment Bertha came by, having found a friend in the person of a bright-eyed young woman of Unity who immediately offered to take my visitors on a tour of Unity campus if I had other things to do and if it would be all right with me. It was. What is it Unity says, "God's wisdom ever guides my way, working His good through me by the power of the Spirit within?"

So we sauntered over to the terrace adjoining the snack bar at the Inn and the seeker suggested we have some sodas even though, Emily insisted, they would probably spoil our lunch. As they were served to us and as we relaxed, Bertha said of things in general, "Isn't it all wonderful!"

The Unity member agreed, referring to the rose garden, the fountains, the quadrangle, the Tower, the people walking by who included a bus load of youngsters on a sightseeing trip.

Leaning back in his chair, the seeker agreed that these were good moments and that the fact that people could play golf on the grounds, could swim in the luxurious pool, and take advantage of lake fishing just a stone's throw away assured him that Unity loved life. Emily, however, had a question for Bertha's newly found friend. "Tell me," she asked, "what were you before you became interested in the Unity movement?"

"What was I?" the young woman asked in surprise.

"I mean," said Emily, "what church did you come out of?"

"Oh, I have always been in Unity," she responded, as if the question had never been asked of her before. "My parents are in Unity, too."

"That's interesting," said the observer, "I suppose that everyone in Unity came from some other religion. And what have you found in Unity?"

"I'm interested in the Sunday School work," was the answer. "Of course, I think Unity has just about the finest Sunday School curriculum in the whole world."

Bertha agreed and explained that before a child is old enough to understand, intellectually, very much about God, he is taught that God is good, that the world is good, that he is surrounded with goodness, that he lives in a friendly universe, and that he is to regard himself as the highest possible expression of goodness.

"Well, now," Emily was forced to say, "that is all very well, but the fact is, the world is not always good and I sometimes wonder about this kind of teaching. Take some of your affirmations—which I have heard Bertha use—they do not always seem right to me. What if I stood on a street corner affirming that I live in a friendly world, full of goodness and all that, as you say, and a car suddenly jumped up on the curb and knocked me down? Seems to me you people are not always realistic."

"Oh," the Unity girl replied, "if you were in perfect harmony with God, you would not be on the corner at that particular moment. Or if you were, no car would come along to knock you down, or if it did there would be some meaning in whatever happened, far beyond your knowing, but eventually for some ultimate good!"

Emily turned to me for help. "Well, I just don't get *that!*" she exclaimed. "Do you?"

"Not all of it, perhaps," I admitted, "but isn't it a wonderful way to live?"

"Right!" agreed the seeker. "I feel as you do, a wonderful way to live."

So we talked for a while about personal experiences which all of us had felt were tragic at the moment and out of which some unusual meaning later emerged. I shared with them the story about the Unity minister who had been victimized and who "got even" with his persecutor by blessing him.

"That, too," the seeker said thoughtfully, "strikes me as a good way to live. When someone double crosses you, bless him and wish him good luck! Maybe that's what was meant by 'turning the other cheek.' If we lived that way it might work some real miracles, and Lord knows the world needs them."

"It may possibly work where the person really believed that way," Emily conceded, "but I am not so sure. God gave us our own judgment to help us deal with these situations. And you simply cannot trust everyone."

"Well," the husband declared, turning a fresh cigar over in his hands, "I think it would work. The whole point is, as you say, a person must believe a thing before he can live it." Then, with his lighter poised he added, "Or maybe he must live it before he can believe it."

"Either way," Bertha chimed in, "or both ways. As long as it works!"

"What brought *you* into Unity?" I asked Bertha, "outside of the fact that 'the fullness of time had come?'"

"I have often wondered just what it was and how it came about," she reflected. "It wasn't the need for physical healing, as it was with many people. Actually it was not really any special need. I think it was simply that the Jesus whom I loved as a child did not satisfy me as an adult. But the consciousness of Christ, the demonstration of God's goodness through Jesus in me by way of this consciousness, this is a truth that has been marvelously satisfying and provable in my life. Then, whenever I went to the services, I found something in them of practical help. I really like Unity services very much. You know, I have the feeling that I am going to church and not going to church when I go to Unity. Do you know what I mean?"

"Well," I said, "Unity has two fields of expression, the lesson and the laboratory. The lesson or church service deals with the exploration of truths and hypotheses, affirmations, and the like. The laboratory side has to do with the application of these truths in life, testing and proving them in the workaday world. It is in this second area that we of the old-line religions are delinquent. We are too often poor doers of the Word."

"That's another thing," the Unity friend observed, "in Unity no one ever fights with God, much less argues with Him. There is no suggestion that God must do this or that for us, that He must be defended or criticized or anything like that. He simply *is*. There is no need to hurry Him or be hurried by Him. He *is*, and that is all that needs to be said."

There was not much that anyone could say in the light of her conviction. Although there might have been questions, there was no doubt that she had the Unity kind of confidence, a "God's-in-His-heaven, all's-right-with-the-world" kind of confidence, and it would have been presumptuous to have asked her to explain or justify it. She was like Unity and Unity was like her, minimizing evil, maximizing God.

Long after we said good-by and I went back to the motel to do my packing, I thought of this Unity spirit and felt like saying, "If it be imagination, let us have more of it, and if it be the power of faith, let us have more faith."

There is room, it seemed to me, for one religion that sets up faith flares along humanity's troubled road and keeps the traffic moving. There is room in the world for one religion that has not only a light touch, but, at times, an almost play-like quality which says, "Things are in divine order," even when they appear not to be. A religion which dares affirm, "Thank God for this apparent reversal in my fortune, for it is not a reversal, it has some deep meaning which will now unfold for me." One religion that says, as I once heard a Unity member say, "Thank God for my aching back! It gives me a chance to prove the divine power of healing." One religion which allows and understands the deeper significance of the phrase that all religion is a quest—for the good.

Since there are so many religious groups which emphasize original sin, let there be one which stresses original virtue. Because there is a preponderance of movements convinced that whom the Lord loveth He chasteneth, let there be one which insists He only blesses those He loves.

It is a big world and there may still not be enough religions to satisfy every type of mind, but let us grant one the right to operate without a theological spokesman determined to defend his position to the death. Let there be one with doctrines no more abstruse than those which are found in a sermon on the mount and no more complex than the life of Him that lived them.

There is room, I concluded, in Christendom's rich and teeming family for one movement which thinks of missions in terms of the Word, of evangelism in terms of a stream of prayer, and of conversion in terms of the discovery of Self. Among the cavalcade of faiths which pay homage to heritage and tradition, let there be one which respects the constant unfoldment of Truth.

One religion there should be that is not interested in statistics or expansion or prestige; a confraternal kind of faith, impartial as to how its ideals are propagated; a modern movement justifying itself on what it has to give, not get, on what it has yet to learn as well as on what it has found, and on what it now is as well as on what it presumes still to become.

And so I affixed a Unity sticker on the visor of my car. It said:

"This is God's car. It neither gives nor receives offense in all its journeyings. God's hand is at the wheel. His wisdom chooses the way. His law of order and right adjustment is manifest in all its mechanism. No fear alarms its occupants; for God's presence blesses them with the spirit of peace."

This, I felt was good for my car and good for me as I prepared to drive away from Unity Village. As I closed the motel door and then sat for a moment in the car, reflecting on my Unity stay, I thought of how, through the years of my research, I have seen religions born, have watched them grow, have seen some die. Most of all, I have seen them take their place in the cultural scene of our country and then level out and get to be "just another denomination."

Far be it from me to predict Unity's destiny or prophesy its future. That is up to Unity. What I do know beyond the shadow of a doubt and what I will predict is that there will always be a faith *like* the Unity I have described, for there is something in the human heart that wants and needs what Unity has to give.

And what is that?

A God of peace, a Son of love, a Spirit of joy.

Peace, love, and joy as the essence of life are, I suppose, the products of Truth, and divine life embraces and encompasses this Truth here and in the life to come.

The drone of the highway traffic grew louder as I drove out of the shrubbery-bordered lane. At the portaled entrance I had to stop and wait my chance to get across the moving stream of cars. A group of Unity visitors in a station wagon waved at me as I was waiting there and one in the party called my name, asking why I was leaving just when he was coming in. Each visitor to Unity brings something in the way of spiritual meaning, and receives something. No one knew better than I what Unity knows so well: you never give a blessing without receiving one. Like the lanes that wind into Unity Village from the highway—they run both ways.

I rarely pick up hitch-hikers, and it may be that if it had been anywhere but at the Unity fruit stand just across the street, I would not have picked up this young man with a suitcase and a sign that said: CHICAGO OR BUST. The timing was right, my mood was right, the young man seemed right. I took him in.

The Saturday traffic was heavy, but the afternoon was bright. In the rear view mirror the Unity Tower appeared to grow ever taller as the land unfolded and the Village receded in the background.

We had just reached a good cruising speed when the young man asked, "What's Unity anyway?"

I adjusted my driver's seat, put the car visor with its blessing in place, and settled back to the rhythm of the road.

"To begin with," I said, "Unity is first of all a way of life."